THE
COVENANT RELATIONSHIP

THE
COVENANT RELATIONSHIP

Henrietta Freeman

XULON PRESS

Xulon Press
2301 Lucien Way #415
Maitland, FL 32751
407.339.4217
www.xulonpress.com

Xulon Press

© 2023 by Henrietta Freeman

Cover Design by XULON PRESS
Edited by Cassandra Kay

All rights reserved solely by the author. The author guarantees all contents are original and do not infringe upon the legal rights of any other person or work. No part of this book may be reproduced in any form without the permission of the author.Due to the changing nature of the Internet, if there are any web addresses, links, or URLs included in this manuscript, these may have been altered and may no longer be accessible. The views and opinions shared in this book belong solely to the author and do not necessarily reflect those of the publisher. The publisher therefore disclaims responsibility for the views or opinions expressed within the work.

Unless otherwise indicated, Scripture quotations taken from the King James Version (KJV)–*public domain.*

Scripture quotations taken from the Holy Bible, New International Version (NIV). Copyright © 1973, 1978, 1984, 2011 by Biblica, Inc.™. Used by permission. All rights reserved.

Scripture quotations taken from the Holy Bible, New Living Translation (NLT). Copyright ©1996, 2004, 2007 by Tyndale House Foundation. Used by permission of Tyndale House Publishers, Inc.

Scripture quotations taken from the New King James Version (NKJV). Copyright © 1982 by Thomas Nelson, Inc. Used by permission. All rights reserved.

Scripture quotations taken from the Amplified Bible (AMP). Copyright © 1954, 1958, 1962, 1964, 1965, 1987 by The Lockman Foundation. Used by permission. All rights reserved.

Paperback ISBN-13: 978-1-66286-326-4
Ebook ISBN-13: 978-1-66286-327-1

DEDICATION

This book is dedicated to those who are planning to get married: I pray that you place God at the center of your marriage and allow Him to lovingly guide you through your new journey of love, and your lifetime commitment as one. For those who are already married: you are the three strand cord that cannot be easily broken. With God at the center of your union, you can overcome any obstacle that tries to come your way, so continue to love and cherish one another; treat each other well in the eyes of the LORD; and continue to protect your sacred union no matter what comes. For those who are single: you are not alone; you are loved and cared for by the Almighty God who loves you unconditionally, and who desires to prepare you mentally and spiritually in a season designed for just you and Him. He also desires to prepare you for the one that He has ordained you to be with; to share in a most beautiful and sacred union of a lifetime.

DEDICATION

TABLE OF CONTENTS

Acknowledgments ix
Preface xi

The Covenant Relationship 1
The First Marriage 27
The Sacred Vows 35
After A Wedding Comes A Marriage 55
Becoming One 71
Understanding The Brokenness We Face 83
Spiritual Wickedness In High Places 93
Give Yourself Permission To Be Single 103
Put No One Above God 127
There Is Power in Unity! 141

Biography 151

ACKNOWLEDGMENTS

I want to first give praise unto my Lord and Savior Jesus Christ! Without you, nothing is possible, but with You, ALL things are made possible! I am grateful for this love journey that I have been fortunate to spend with You. Thank you for never giving up on me. You are faithful and you have proven time and time again that you will never leave me, nor will you forsake me. You are my everything and I am nothing without you. If I lost everything I had, I still have everything that I will ever need in this life because I have You. You are the greatest love of my life!

To my Mom, I love you. Thank you for just simply being who you are and for being there to give me those special talks when I needed them the most. God bless you always! And to both my Dads: Bobby and Henry, I love you dearly.

Apostle Ric and Pastor Brenda Martin of Change With A Praise Ministry, I truly thank God for the both of you! I can testify to how mightily God has used the both of you during my time at CWAPM. Not only have you shown how transparent you are, but you both truly exemplify God's love for His people. You both have a heart for loving and serving the people of God and it shows in all that you do. I am grateful for you both being in my life and for all that you have help to impart within me. May the Lord continue to bless you both in every aspect of your lives, in great abundance. I love you both.

To Cierra and Jalen, you both have blessed me in your own unique ways. At times I can see how the Lord ministers through the both of you, without you even realizing it. I love you both and may God continue to bless you and raise you up in Him to be used for His glory.

To my sisters, Mary, Bobbie, and Sharon, each of you are such a blessing in your own way. Thanks for always being there in every way that you are. Continue to allow God to have His way in each of your lives; being a great blessing to others. To my recently departed brother Jimmy, I know you're smiling down on me from heaven.

Cassandra Kay, to know you, is to be blessed by you. Mighty Woman of God, I can't thank you enough for being such a great blessing in my life! God was extremely generous in blessing you in every way that He has. I look forward to God releasing the work of your hands because it will be a blessing to many! Keep being the mighty soldier for God that you are. No eye has seen, nor ear heard of the plans God has for you! God bless you abundantly. Love you.

To my other family members; friends; colleagues; and the women's ministry, thank you so much for your encouragement, prayers, and support. While I cannot personally thank everyone by name, please know that you are in my heart and I love you. May God bless you All.

PREFACE

A covenant can be described as promise between two or more individuals. The parties involved make a binding promise that they will work together to achieve a common goal. Covenants can have conditions, which can involve stipulations with consequences. To enter into a sacred covenant such as marriage, one must know of the importance of being willing to commit to such a sacred promise.

Years ago, I made a mistake in taking the sacredness of the covenant of marriage for granted. Upon learning from my mistakes and learning about the sanctity of this sacred union, I want to encourage others to be sober minded as they consider entering into such a sacred promise, not only with one another but with God. The message that is being relayed throughout this book, is a message that was first given unto me from the LORD. The covenants of the Bible can help us to understand the importance of entering into such a sacred promise with God. Here are just a few examples of the many covenants of the Bible:

The Edenic Covenant refers to the covenant that was made between God and Adam. This covenant takes place in the Garden of Eden, and it represents a time of innocence. Adam was given responsibility to obey God and in turn God would bless him with abundant life (Genesis 1:26-30). It also focuses on the responsibility that was given to Adam. He had been given dominion over all the earth and over all the creatures of the earth. He had an obligation to tend to the Garden; to replenish the earth, as well as subdue it. He was also warned of the tree of knowledge of good and evil (Genesis 2:15-17).

The Adamic Covenant focuses on Adam's timeframe in the Garden of Eden. Adam had the responsibility to obey and uphold his agreement with God. If Adam would have pondered on the results of his obedience to God, it should have been enough to make him avoid any disobedience. This covenant was dependent upon Adam's obedience, but when Adam and Eve ate from the tree of knowledge of good and evil, it can be said that through one man, sin entered the world (Romans 5:12). Adam was the headship and a representation for all people. When Adam fell, the entire human race fell. We were all in the body of Adam when he sinned. The serpent that tempted Eve was cursed and God promised redemption through the seed of the woman (Genesis 3:6, 14-15).

Under the Noahic Covenant, Noah finds grace with God. God told Noah that He will establish His covenant with him (Genesis 6:8, 18-22). When Man failed under the Adamic covenant, people began to continuously commit such evil acts, which caused God to judge them with the Flood. God told Noah to make an Ark and to bring with him, his wife, his sons and their wives, and every living thing; two of every sort and after its kind; male and female. This was Noah's command, which he was obedient to. After the Flood, the promise to mankind was that God would never again use a flood to destroy all life. God has given us rainbows in the sky as a sign of His kept promise to us. He also promises that while the earth remains, there will be seedtime and harvest, and the cycles of the seasons will continue (Genesis 8:20-22).

The Abrahamic Covenant refers to the covenant that God made with Abraham. Under this covenant, God promised to make Israel a great nation. He also promised Abraham that He would bless his seed and make his name great, and in turn Abraham would be made a blessing. God promised to bless those who blessed Abraham and curse those who cursed him. God's promise included giving him the

Promised Land (Genesis 12:1-3, 7). Through his descendants, would eventually come a Redeemer. The covenant would also extend to Isaac and Jacob as well.

The Mosaic Covenant involved God's chosen leader of Israel–Moses. God promised to be with Moses as he led the children of Israel out of the captivity of Pharaoh. God promises to redeem the children of Israel. God established the covenant with Israel by letting the children of Israel know that "you will be my people and I will be your God" (Exodus 6:6-7). Here, God speaks to Moses and tells him to tell the children of Israel: Exodus 19:5-6 (KJV) *Now therefore, if ye will obey my voice indeed, and keep my covenant, then ye shall be a particular treasure unto me above all people for all the earth is mine: And ye shall be unto me a kingdom of priests, and an holy nation."*

The Davidic Covenant refers to the promise to David: a kingdom without an end which would ultimately be fulfilled by Jesus Christ. David was chosen by God and anointed to be king by Samuel. God made many promises to David such as to be with David as he went out to defeat his enemies; a promise to be a great name; and a promise to establish the kingdom of David's offspring. There are 3 specific features that make up the ongoing Davidic covenant: a house; a kingdom; and a throne (2 Samuel 7:8-16).

The New Covenant involves the promise to Mankind that God will forgive the sins of all who accepted and believes in His Son Jesus Christ. Under this new covenant, God will set aside a people for Himself from all the nations of the earth to form the bride of Christ. The most important part of this covenant is the blood of Jesus Christ, which was shed for the remissions of our sins. Jesus provided his own body as a sacrifice once and for all who would believe on Him. Because of His everlasting love, we can all receive the gift of salvation and even the presence of the Holy Spirit freely (Jeremiah 31:31-34).

THE COVENANT RELATIONSHIP

There are many reasons people decide to get married. For several decades, values and morals have changed within cultures and societies, and some of these results has had negative effects on the institution of marriage. No longer do people see marriage as a covenant, but these days, you will find that more people marry for the convenience of being married.

Nowadays, many people tend to view marriage as a contract that can be easily broken at any time and for whatever reason, especially when the relationship no longer meets their needs. It can be summed up that some people may lack what constitutes a bona-fide marriage. Some may even lack the ability to honor one's word; commitment; and dedication held in covenant between two people and their God.

Even though love plays a significant role in the decision, what stands out more is one's ability to do what honors the institution and the primary clause in the vows spoken, which is, "Until death, do we part". Those 5 words are the clause of evidence that no matter what happens, we have a covenant of agreement. The covenant is the agreement that denotes the stipulations on which the two decide that they shall live as one union, which signifies the genuineness of the relationship. Amos 3:3 (KJV) states, *"Can the two walk together except they be agreed"*.

A covenant regarding marriage, is an agreement that is to be solemn, and even sacred. You will find that in most faith-practiced beliefs, a covenant is a promise, or an agreement made by God with mankind. God explains His expectations and stipulates where His decisions are founded upon unconditional love. He is aware of and He takes into consideration the weakness of man, but not deviating from His promises, He keeps His word. God never broke or compromised His promises with those He entered into an agreement with. God is a covenant keeper.

Deuteronomy 7:9 (KJV) states, *"Know therefore that the Lord thy God, He is God, the faithful God, which keepeth covenant and mercy with them that love Him and keep His commandments to a thousand generations"*. Just imagine God keeping His covenant promises to a thousand generations; this is truly His love and grace that deserves admiration and heeding to His instructions.

Nonetheless, many marriages of today are barely surviving their 10-year anniversary, yet alone a 5-year anniversary. Celebrating a 30, 40, or even 50 year wedding anniversary is almost rare these days, and by the way, if you know someone who has made it to this mark, be sure to congratulate them! If they give you any wisdom, listen up, because those words of advice could surely be the words of victory that hurdles you through the next challenge in your arena of matrimony.

For those who are planning to get married, I truly believe that the LORD desires that we understand the sacredness and sanctity of this powerful union of a covenant relationship (marriage) and how it involves Him. He doesn't want us to enter into such a sacred promise lightly, but to have an understanding of the promise that we will partake in as a solemn vow.

When someone considers marriage, it's important to take the time to evaluate how sacred this union can truly be since God has a voice in this decision and when He reveals His plans, one must ask himself if he is willing to obey the voice of God. The response should be "yes", especially if you are faithfully seeking Him for guidance and have a readiness and willingness to obey. Upon realizing the seriousness of a covenant union, there could be less divorces and perhaps more people willing to find the extended grace within themselves to forgive and work through the rough patches of a marriage.

Looking back on my past mistakes regarding my marriage, I now believe that the LORD tolerated me in my weaknesses. He has recently allowed me to be on a journey to discover what it really means to enter into a covenant agreement. Today, when I think about a covenant, I think of a very special and sacred union; it is now to me, an everlasting bond.

It has been by test and trial that God allowed me to see that He answered my prayers and gave me a husband, but at the time I was not prepared to be a covenant wife. I could not mirror the aspect of a covenant as presented in the Bible by an all loving; great, and wonderful God. Though I was learning about God, I was not learning much about myself in times past. I believed I wanted to be a wife but I did not know the essence or qualities of being involved in a covenant relationship. I did not know how to be honest and trustworthy; I only expected to receive it. I did not know the validity of my promises that were needed in order that my spouse could be enhanced and strengthened.

I was married years ago, and upon preparing for that marriage, my mind and heart were not in the right place. I took my vows and the person I married for granted. Nothing motivated me to become a covenant wife; even going to marriage counseling, I still did not fully take the position of my commitment as being sacred. Seriously, I was being foolish, and because of the foolishness that was in my heart at the time, it caused my marriage to be over before it ever started.

I am compelled to write and share my experience, in hopes that someone else will learn from my mistakes as well as avoid the pitfalls and the pain of divorce. I also hope that through the revelation and information that I have shared will encourage others who are planning to enter into such a sacred union; that they will understand the serious commitment that it will take to commit to making their marriage work.

Throughout the Bible, in the Old Testament scriptures, you can see how marriage is used as an allegory of God's relationship with His people, Israel. Israel's disobedience to God can be viewed like a wayward spouse. Although Israel was unfaithful, God remained faithful in His love and commitment of the covenant that He made with His people, Israel.

Despite my waywardness, my husband may have given up on me but God never gave up on His committed love covenant with me. People have the tendency to love with conditions because they tend to love from the place of how they have been taught what love is. I praise God because He loves us unconditionally despite our sins. Though I did not honor the covenant of my promise with my husband and God, I know that God forgave me. However, though forgiven, it doesn't mean that God did not deal with me of how I handled things with my marriage.

Though we are now under the covenant of grace, we still shall reap what seeds we planted in someone else's life. Galatians 6:7 (KJV) states "Be not deceived; God is not mocked: for whatsoever a man soweth, that shall he also reap." Even though I did not keep my promise to my husband in honoring my vows, "until death do we part", God kept His promise to me, in promising to never leave me, nor forsake me. He promised to love and redeem me.

Years ago when I was in my late 20's, I remember praying to the LORD for a husband. I was frustrated with dating the wrong kind of men. Some of the relationships I was involved in were horrible, and also abusive. I remember I started growing sick and tired of the dating scene and I desired to meet a great guy and settle down.

In 2004, I remember working for a certain company and that is where I met a man who initially worked in the same department as I did. I had not noticed him right away but I must have evidently caught his eye because one day, he made his way over to me to introduce himself. He told me that his name was Derrick and he asked of my name and I told him. He had a nice smile. He began small talk with me, for instance, he would talk about the job and inquired if I liked working there. This of course led to other discussions. He was definitely not short of any conversation: he had the gift of gab. Yet, he had my attention because he had great conversation, along with many jokes.

I remember how he made me laugh. Laughter is one of the ways to my heart; I love comedy and laughter. I had a deep appreciation for his ability to make me smile and laugh. It was not an attempt to flatter me, he just only wanted to make sure my days were filled with joy. Though I could tell that there was an age gap between the two of us, but at the time I was unaware of the difference in the years. However, I really enjoyed having talks with him while at work; he definitely made the time go by quickly.

The more Derrick and I became acquainted, the more his interest in me grew. He eventually asked for my phone number. We exchanged numbers and we would end up talking on the phone for hours each time. He was very funny and he had a lot of wisdom. Information should be shared, and he was never reluctant about sharing what he knew in order to help me.

In addition to Derrick's compassion, humor, and wisdom, he also loved God. He was always excited about sharing his testimony, for he genuinely appreciated God for his deliverance from drugs. He knew God's love prevailed over his addiction and changed his life. Whenever he shared the goodness of God's love, he would always tell of his rescue from a life of destruction.

He would not hold back on letting you know just how deep his involvement with drugs went and how grateful he was that God never gave up on him. He came to understand the wealth of God's mercy; the value of God's investment of Jesus Christs' sacrifice; and the unconditional love that drove him to want to love in a great capacity.

The more I got to know Derrick, the more I felt at ease with him. I was able to fully be myself with him and I could unfold my box before him without any shame. Most of the time, people tend to want you to hear their story, but as a true friend he also listened to mine. We shared our stories, our past and present situations that either helped us to grow or hindered our pace.

Derrick became important to me, like one of my closet friends. Our friendship was reciprocated beyond conversations. Whenever he needed help, I didn't mind doing things for him. I can remember him asking me one day if I could pick up his clothes from the dry cleaners. Derrick had so much to do that day that he couldn't make it on time before the dry cleaners closed. He did not ask a lot, but whenever he did ask, I certainly did not mind. I wanted to assure him that I was just as much a friend to him as he was being to me. He had become someone that I really cared about as a close friend.

We would meet up for lunch or dinner on the weekends and would even visit each other's church. Derrick treated me with the upmost respect. He cared for me, and his concern was not hidden. He was very much interested about my personal matters and he certainly didn't mind doing things for me.

He had an element of chivalry, and he wanted me to know how much he believed I deserved to be respected. Simple things that have faded from the normal behaviors of men, such as opening doors, was not an issue for him. If I needed anything, he wanted to provide it. He was very thoughtful; and he cherished the woman in me.

I eventually allowed him to meet my children. He took a liking to them and they seem to like him too. Derrick was great with them. My children thought he was the funniest man they ever met. As much as he made me laugh, he would have the kids laughing even harder. He would do things for them that their own dad wasn't doing for them at the time. If I had a financial need for my children, he would give me money to help buy them whatever they needed; even on a holiday or just preparing them for the first day of school, he made sure that they were provided for.

My children really appreciated the efforts that Derrick had made for them and they enjoyed him being around. I would invite him to have dinner with us and the quality of our friendship was always exemplified before my children. He never took advantage of our space. We had some great times; we carried on and did all of this as just simply being friends.

After some time had passed, our friendship had blossomed into something unique, but I realized Derrick began to desire more from me. He was becoming committed to more than I was prepared for. I had avoided his implied statements of wanting to move beyond friendship. He seemed to have had a lot of self-control in the beginning, but eventually Derrick confessed the fact that he was interested in more than being friends. I had always wondered if men and women could truly be friends and remain as only friends. I had always wanted a male friend, and prior to Derrick, those friendships would sadly come to an end because the men would always desire more.

This friendship was different, or so I thought. I kept Derrick in the friend zone for a long time. When Derrick told me that he was interested in me and wanted to pursue a relationship, I turned him down. I told him that I thought he was too old for me. He was 23 years older than I was. He didn't look or act old or anything, I just felt that I could not get past the fact that he was much older than I was.

I was never really interested in men who were 5 or more years older than I was. I was 27 when I met Derrick. I truly cared about him and would do anything for him except date him. I always enjoyed my time with him, no matter what we did or where we went. I always felt like he had my best interest in mind on how he cared about me and the things he would do to express his caring ways for me and vice versa. I had Derrick's best interest in mind when I did things for him to show that I cared for him. I enjoyed our friendship so much and I definitely didn't want anything to come between that.

Sometimes I think that when you are genuinely giving of your time and concern to a man, they can think that that's an invitation to be more than friends and that's certainly not what I wanted Derrick to perceive of my kindness towards him. I was adamant about our boundaries, and for the time being, he accepted that we would just remain as friends.

He never forced himself on me, nor did he compromise our values by becoming intimate with me. He was a gentleman and he respected me. Even though he was open about pursuing a relationship with me, I would remind him it could not happen. I refrained from allowing our involvement to become anything more than a friendship. For the most part, he continued to have a great attitude towards me. He even continued to be patient with my decision.

Even more time had passed, and Derrick still continued with patience until one day, I stopped by his house and he was standing outside with a particular look on his face. I got out of the car and inquired about the strange look on his face. I asked him what was wrong. He told me that he and God was waiting on me to make a decision. It's almost like he was trying to say he was growing weary of waiting on me. Derricks' heart was definitely in the right place and he believed God had answered his prayers of finding a wife to love.

He believed God was giving him favor in me. He wanted to convey a message that would change the perspective of our friendship. I asked him what he meant by this and he sat me down and had a long conversation with me. He said, "you prayed for a husband didn't you"? And I said "yes". He was like, "well then, why do you think I'm here"? I heard the question but I could not balance the weight of its worth. I was stunned by what he said but I was not shocked.

In the depth of my spirit, I felt that he may have been the person that God had sent to me. He was the one to be my husband, but you know sometimes when God answer our prayers, it may be a little different from that which we anticipated. I did not convey to him that I too, believed this was orchestrated by God.

I had a problem. I was stubborn and I knew it. I knew what I wanted! In my mind, I knew *what* I wanted my husband to be like. I certainly wanted my husband to be within my age group and if Derrick was what God was giving me, I surely did not appreciate God's plan. I was being difficult, selfish, and ungrateful.

After having that talk with Derrick, I told him that I would rather stay friends with him because I wasn't comfortable with our age difference. He didn't realize it but his age had a great impact on my decision. Being mature for my age, I still did not desire an older man. People often told me that I have an old soul. I am the youngest of 4 daughters and people often were confused because I acted as mature as my sisters were.

There was no issue of communicating with Derrick on his level; I just wasn't into older men. Derrick explained to me that age shouldn't matter. He may have been right in regards to love, because love in its own worth have no stipulation of age, yet my reasoning did not suffice, and it hurt him that the only issue would be a matter of our age.

I wasn't mature enough to handle this situation at the time. When I told him I had a problem with our age difference, I knew that I had hurt his feelings. I wasn't trying to hurt him, I was just being as honest as I knew how, and for me it was the age gap. In wanting his pain to dissipate, I made the attempt to set him up with one of my older sisters, but he was relentless in his feelings for me and he was sure that I was the one God had given to him.

Since he was trusting God, I knew I had to get to a place of hearing from God for myself. I talked with God about this situation. I told God that I just didn't think I could get past this age issue in my mind. Derrick was a good man and I knew he deserved someone to love him the way he deserved to be loved, but I just didn't think I was the one.

I truly did care about him in every way that you could care about a good friend but the attraction to be involved in a relationship as such just wasn't there. He never admitted it but I knew the conversation we had, had hurt him deeply; so eventually he began to distant himself from me and we began seeing less and less of one another.

We weren't talking as much on the phone and we rarely saw each other on the weekends anymore. It hurt me because I wanted my friend back. I wanted my laughing buddy back. Things just didn't seem the same without Derrick. I thought if only he could understand and just be willing to accept my friendship, then things would be alright.

Some time had passed and we ran into each other again and we had a long conversation about how things had been recently going in our lives. It's like we picked up right where we left off and like no time had passed at all. We knew that we had missed each other and had missed hanging out together so after running back into one another, we started hanging out more again and I was just happy to have my friend back in my life.

Over time, my desire for a mate had begun growing more and more intense and I remember talking with Derrick about it. He would keep throwing hints that what I was desiring was right in front of my face but because of my prejudice and stubbornness, I couldn't even see it. So I prayed and prayed about it. I even prayed asking my Holy FATHER, "if this be your will LORD, help me look past the age issue and my selfish desires and receive what you're trying to give me". I eventually pondered with the idea of what could happen if I said yes.

We remained friends for a while longer, but one day I began to think of Derrick, and I told myself to just give it a try. I told myself if it doesn't work, at least you tried. One day while talking with Derrick, I told him that I would be willing to give a relationship with him a try to see if we could really connect on that level. Little did I know, a line was about to be crossed that we would never be able to return to.

We began dating and at first it seemed really weird because I was so accustomed to having Derrick as a friend and now it felt awkward kissing my good friend. It really took some getting used to for me, but Derrick didn't have any problems whatsoever! He was happy and enjoying himself all along the way. As we dated, he continued to be a really great guy. He took the euphoria to another level and I could tell that he really enjoyed making me happy. He would take me to plays out of town and we would enjoy different restaurants that I liked. He continued to open doors for me and would be mindful of the things that I needed.

He was proving himself to be a dependable person in many ways, but I believed that I just did not deserve a great man as Derrick. Subconsciously, I had convinced myself I was not worthy of such a good man. I could not answer the harder question; was it only because of his age that hindered me previously? I could only resort to thinking he deserved better. He deserved a woman that would see past his age and see the contents of his heart. He deserved someone that could appreciate the magnitude of love he was offering.

Then it happened: not long after Derrick and I began dating, surprisingly he had went out and purchased one of the most beautiful rings I had ever seen. He took me out to dinner and to a play, and afterwards, he proposed and I accepted. I got so caught up in the moment and I was happy but I was happy for all the wrong reasons.

I got excited about the possibility to plan a wedding. Planning a wedding should not have been the first thing on my mind but I got caught up in the planning ideas and what my dress would look like, that I had not thought about the real reason I said yes. If Derrick would have paid more attention to where my thought process was, this should have been a red flag for him, but he had been so elated that my response was yes!

When you become engaged, joy can positively overtake your reasoning; yet, if the entire basis of those thoughts is for the mere excitement, then it is time to re- evaluate the reason behind saying "yes". My thought process should have been on focusing on the reality of the love that was established between us and the thought of spending forever with him, but sadly this was not the case. What we meant to each other, should have been the foundation of my desire to be with him, but my thoughts were on everything else but the commitment, dedication, and servitude of a wife.

We told our family and friends about the engagement. My family was happy for me and they told me that I had a great guy. In the days that followed, I began to plan for my wedding. I was excited through the roof as I was able to plan detail by detail of what I wanted. I had always wondered what it would be like to plan a wedding, so I became so consumed with planning the wedding that I wasn't checking my heart to make sure that I was truly in love with this man before going through with the wedding. I did not ask myself to be true to my own heart, nor did I second guess where my morals and values were at this point. All I was aware of at the time was that my role would allow me to walk down an aisle, speak some vows and proclaim I am married.

Though we sought pre-marital counseling, I still refused to answer the tough questions that came through my intuition. During the pre-marital counseling, I had the opportunity to approach some areas of concern, but our Pastor did not assess the waters and neither did I bring up my concerns. Yet it was the perfect time for me to mention my fears; worries; and to be truthful about the age issue that I had with Derrick.

I think my biggest fear of the age issue was that I was afraid of Derrick growing old ahead of me and not growing old with me. I did not think it would be fair to have him only for a specific time and then he precedes me in death. This was a major issue that I had but sadly I kept quiet about this concern and never disclosed it during our counseling sessions. I was wrong on so many levels because I was not only deceiving my heart, but I could not commit to be openly honest with Derrick's heart. My decision was to continue with the wedding plans despite my worries.

I remember keeping a diary of all that was happening in my life and how I was feeling during these times. I didn't know how things would turn out with Derrick and I have to admit that I had many doubts along the way. Keeping a record of my thoughts gave me an outlet of all that I was feeling during this time of uncertainty.

Prior to the wedding, I began working for another company. While working at the company, I met a man named Greg. We worked on a project together and immediately, we disagreed about our personal work habits, performances, and skills to perform our tasks. I remember how we butted heads all the time and we could never agree completely on a project that was assigned for us to collaborate on.

This guy got on my last nerves to the point where I even asked the boss to place me on another assignment. Greg and I couldn't get along in the beginning, but eventually we were able to put our differences aside and work together productively and professionally. It took a while but we overcame our differences and focused on the job that needed completion.

As time went along, I noticed how Greg and I would engage in certain conversations and we even found ourselves laughing and getting along a lot better than we could have even imagined. Our concentration on work projects began to even flow much smoother. There was less arguing amongst us now and with the friction out of the way, we had allowed ourselves to get to know one another better.

One day I found myself looking at Greg in a unique way. I began to find him even more attractive, because I admit that when I first met him, I was like wow, he is handsome, but by us not getting along much in the beginning, I wasn't too focused on his looks. I even began to develop some unexplainable feelings towards him. But wait Henrietta, aren't you engaged? Will you not be getting married soon? The spirit of lust began to take over and I began imaging myself with Greg. He was around my age and extremely attractive. The more we spent time at work, the more I was desiring to spend time with him after work.

To my surprise, I picked up on feelings of attraction from him as well. This was certainly not good. This was a recipe for disaster. I remembered writing about this experience in my diary. I wrote of how I thought about him during the day and how I fantasized about spending time with him.

I could not believe I was carrying on like this – I was engaged and planning a wedding for Christ sake! This was wrong on so many levels! I kept thinking, how could I do this to Derrick! Normally when I am involved in a relationship, I am committed. I'm not one of those people that cheat and mess around while dating someone, therefore, this behavior of mine was taking me by surprise. All I know is that my lust for this other guy was overwhelming and growing stronger and stronger daily.

The evidence of temptation started to taunt me, and I began to have a crazy thought. The thought was coercing me to just give in to my desires and have some fun before saying "I do". I would then try to further convince myself that "no one will ever know". These are the dark voices that try to persuade us that what we do in the dark will never come to see the light of day – but that is far from the truth because what you do in the dark will eventually come to the light. No matter how it is exposed, it eventually comes out. Jesus, Himself gave explanation of this matter in Luke 12:2-3 (KJV) *"For there is nothing covered, that shall not be revealed; neither hid, that shall not be known. Therefore whatsoever ye have spoken in darkness shall be heard in the light; and that which ye have spoken in the ear in closets shall be proclaimed upon the housetops."*

I took pleasure to heeding unto the temptation about Greg. I was giving in and my curiosity had to be satisfied. I wanted to know what it was about him that intrigued me enough to draw my attention away from Derrick. So as I played the game with Greg, I never imagined that Derrick would find out. I didn't tell anyone what I was doing. I was ashamed of myself and felt horrible of what I was doing to Derrick, all for the sake of having fun while at the job. But I couldn't have my cake and eat it too; I was aware of that matter, however, I was also taking down notes of this in my diary.

Derrick eventually moved in with me to help save some money since we were now planning a wedding. At the time, it just made sense for us because in a couple of months we would be getting married. While we were now living together, he would cook and watch the kids while I was at work in the evenings because I had a second shift job at the time.

So the flirting on the job continued, day after day, week after week, month after month. I never saw Greg outside the job but the way we felt about each other was evident that things were gearing up to take a turn for the worst. Those lustful feelings that Greg and I had for one another began to intensify and we started wondering what it would be like with each other if we got together outside the job.

Greg knew I was engaged and questioned why I was planning to go through with the marriage since I had feelings for him. I couldn't give him a straight answer. Derrick was mature and had the stability that I needed but Greg had that young, hot appeal and attractiveness that I preferred; which was something I found missing with Derrick.

Derrick had what I desired of a man but I was struggling with fighting the lustful temptations that I had for Greg. I wasn't turned on for Derrick the way I was for Greg and all I could remember is that I wanted that fire. I desired that fervor in my relationship with Derrick but it just wasn't there.

I had to ask myself, what's more important; having a really hot guy with fire and passion, or having a stable, mature man who knows about life and was ready to make a commitment? A man like Derrick who cared for me and captured my essence; a man who allowed God's love to resonate in his heart for me; and a man who loved me from my most inner being beyond any of my shortcomings. If only I had really thought on these things, I would have never allowed my feelings to go there for Greg.

These questions flooded my mind and yet I could not be honest within to answer based on need instead of lustful desires. My youthful mindset interrupted my ability to be the woman I was. I was making an unhealthy decision. I knew better and negated my ability to seek God and ask Him to rescue me from myself.

If you ask me that question today, of course I would have made the better choice for my actions, decisions, and presumptions, but this is where the young, dumb and immature mentality of mine kicked in because I should have known better. If I could go back in time, of course I would have made better decisions without a doubt.

I knew that Greg was not the right person for me, nor could he have been there for me the way that Derrick was, but I was being driven away by the lust of my flesh. It was sad because at the time, I didn't recognize or understand this logic the way that I do today. I was burning with passion for Greg and all I know is that I wanted to be with him.

The right thing for me to have done at that moment would have been to call off the wedding but I never did. The wedding plans were already underway. The date was set; the dress was bought; the tux was rented; the wedding party was getting prepared, and so was the decorations. I thought, I've come too far to turn back now and I did not want to jeopardize losing one of my dearest friends which was now my fiancé. I didn't know what to do. I was so conflicted and I couldn't believe all of this was happening. I just kept thinking, how did I get here? I know it was the lust of my flesh that brought me to the place of betrayal and deceit.

I cannot prove it and Derrick never admitted it, but the days leading up to the wedding, I felt like he was discerning things about me that wasn't right. Even today, I still don't know why he stood by his decision to go ahead and marry me. I feel that in the back of his mind he knew that I wasn't truly in love with him and maybe he thought things would change once we were married.

The week leading up to the wedding ceremony, unbelievably, I made the most stupid decision of my life. Earlier, I mentioned how Greg and I had only been flirting with each other at work but we toiled with the decision to eventually meet outside of work. The week of my wedding, I was pressured by the burning questions running through my mind, and so I finally gave in to my lust and chose to meet Greg outside of work. Yes, the day before my wedding! I could have met him any other time but I chose the day before. What was I thinking?!

Again, those dark thoughts in my head just kept saying, "go meet Greg to see what it would be like to be with him before the opportunity is lost forever"! Indeed, I was listening to the wrong voices in my head and I eventually gave in to them. I met up with Greg and we embraced in some passionate kisses. He wanted to go further but that was as far as I went because even though I gave in to my lustful desires of being with him, my conscious would not agree to let me go any further. It's crazy how I chose the wrong time to start listening to my sub-conscious! Had I listened earlier on, things would have never progressed this far.

Did I regret my decision to meet with Greg-yes! I regretted it and hated myself for doing this to Derrick. As my conscious got the best of me, I stormed out of Greg's house and never looked back. Derrick did not deserve this and I didn't deserve a man like Derrick. As I think about that time past, I can say that I was young and dumb, but all I could think about was fulfilling my own selfish desires. The show and tell of a relationship that could have been honored with holy matrimony was now smeared with deceit; lust; and lies. My heart was far from being truly in love with Derrick and dedicated to him as the one I was planning to commit to and call my husband.

I was not ready to be the kind of wife that Derrick needed: the kind of wife established in covenant with him. I was far from being a virtuous woman; I wasn't even on the radar. I did not completely understand the fullness of what it took to be a wife. I should have been open, honest, and able to stand up and tell Derrick the truth and called the wedding off. Now that being said, if he had the love of God in his heart for me as he claimed, perhaps he would have forgiven my in the moment and we could have entered into a covenant-based marriage with no deceit or lies.

The day of our wedding came, and Derrick and I got married. It was a beautiful ceremony and a great time to spend with family and friends by our side. As I stood at the altar saying my vows, I didn't fully understand the meaning of my vows; to me, they were just words that I uttered for the performance of the ceremony.

Later on this journey of salvation, I asked myself, "What audacity I had to disregard the sacredness of holy matrimony"? How dare I take my vows to the LORD in vain! How dare I take such a sacred covenant in vain! Not only did I stand before a congregation of onlookers, but I stood before a Holy God; and stated words by which I was trusted to perform until death that my husband and I would depart.

Looking back now, it sickens me to my stomach that I took my vows before the LORD in vain. At the time I wasn't fully aware of how sacred of a covenant agreement marriage was and yet I entered into this agreement with sacred vows. My word I had given and later realized I could not hold up to it. I just remember how glad I was to be in the moment with my family and friends; grinning from ear to ear.

As we settled into our now married life, I still felt the same way towards Derrick but my feelings towards Greg began to disappear. We still worked together, but now in separate departments. I was glad that I didn't sleep with Greg but I still regretted ever meeting up with him the day before my wedding.

Sure, you can say that I was an awful person and I have to totally agree with you. My promises was a facade; for hidden in my heart was an unbearable truth – I did not think I should have married Derrick. Even though I was spinning out of control with my behavior and being selfish, I was grateful that God had mercy on me regarding the things that I did to Derrick.

I wrote down so much of my experiences in my diary and I stashed the diary where I did not think no one would ever find it. Remember how I said what you do in the dark will eventually come to the light? Well the dirt that I did in the dark was about to come to the light. During this time, my relationship with the LORD was not as strong as it is today. I knew little about discernment and how secret things could be revealed to people about the type of things that could be going on. Never would I ever have thought that Derrick would find my diary!

There was a time before we were married that I had suspected Derrick knew something was going on with me. I thought that maybe he had suspected my discretion beforehand, but if he did, why did he not confront me about the issue? Why did he allow me to carry on, and marry me anyway? Did he marry me for his own selfish reasons? These are some of the thoughts that later flooded my mind about Derrick.

Not only did Derrick find my diary, but he actually read it. If there was any flaw in Derrick, it had now been discovered. He didn't say anything to me at first but I remember one day he kept watching me very strangely. He had this strange and mean look on his face as he watched me but he never said a word.

One night, in the middle of the night while I was sleeping, he woke me up and started yelling and fussing at me. Clearly I could see that he was extremely upset, but the words that began to come out of his mouth clearly let me know that he had read my diary. What I came to realize, as good of a man that Derrick was, he still was not perfect. His heart was destroyed because he allowed any doubt of my love for him to be eradicated with the simple "Yes" that I gave him.

He was hurt, and sometimes when we trust that God has made provisions for our petitions; we ask ourselves in a subliminal question to God, the how and the why. I could not read the context of his anger, but I do know the man I had married was not the one on display. How could he not just forgive me and move on with a quiet discussion? I was not trying to justify his behavior but I had to make sense of his pain.

I knew I was the one who had done this terrible thing to him. I hurt him without any justification. I stood toe-to-toe with him and promised I would love him and would continue to do so until death did we part. I infringed upon his good will to honor me, provide for me, and most of all love me for better or worst. Those are sacred things that make couples persevere 10, 20, and some even 50 years under the guidance and declaration of a holy matrimony.

I was speechless. I couldn't say anything to him. Everything that came out of his mouth was correct and everything he called me, I somehow deserved it. I never meant to hurt Derrick. I got caught up in lust and what I thought I wanted for a moment. I don't think Derrick was only hurt from just reading my diary and finding out personal thoughts that I had about him and thoughts that I had about Greg, but I believe he had suppressed the truth about my feelings for him and hoped for a better outcome, such as I could grow to love him the way he desired me to.

Surely, I loved him but I was not in love with him. Surely I wanted to be a wife, but I was in no way his covenant wife. Though he sensed these things, he had a greater hope that marrying me would turn these things for our good. While we were just friends, I would admit to him things about my past relationships and how I felt about certain men because we would discuss men and women and the things we liked and did not like as far as relationships are concerned. I gave him specific information and yet in capturing my essence, he overlooked my flaws.

Love can blind anyone because love looks beyond faults and discovers potential for our better person. Maybe he thought that he would always come in second place to another guy or would just never be what I had truly desired. We both settled for the uncertainty of what the marriage could bring us. Now remember, he placed his trust in God, but at that time I did not know how to walk with God. I definitely did not know how to walk with a God-fearing man. I think he wanted to be that guy who exemplified loving your wife as Christ loves the church, but in his own ability to constrain his pain, he lashed out and expressed with anger, hurt, and pain of how he felt.

We should have gone before the LORD with a petition to be honest, and to have a heart to forgive. I do not think it mattered to him that Greg and I did not sleep with one another, I believe the betrayal itself to be charmed and follow through with lustful desires broke all we had promised we would not do.

Derrick never should have been forced to endure this kind of pain from me or anyone else for that matter. He was genuine in his faith and in his love and I broke him in ways that I could not fix. He should never have had to feel like he wasn't good enough or that he was lacking in some area. I hate that I hurt him the way I did because he never deserved that. The promises that Derrick made to me before we were married of how he would be an understanding husband; one who would be willing to work out any problems; one who would provide for the home; and one who would love his wife for better or worse, had now been long forgotten.

While being married to Derrick, I began to see the promises that he made to me decrease time after time. Now all of a sudden, I was responsible for using my own money to pay majority of the bills and so on. I was now being made responsible for things that the head of the household would normally be responsible for. He just seemed to display an "I don't care attitude" towards me and our marriage.

I don't know if the attitude that Derrick now displayed towards me were out of spite for how I had hurt him, or was he always like this and had told me what he thought I wanted to hear, just so that I would marry him. Either way, he quickly forgot about the vows that he had shared with me and he began to act in such a way that left him unrecognizable.

I remember one day, we got into such an intense argument, and after that argument things were never the same between us and we eventually separated; a year later, we filed for divorce. We both walked away willingly from our vows and commitment that we had made to each other and to God.

Even after several years had gone by, I knew that we could never be friends again. I had longed to have that friendship back with him but I knew it was impossible. I honestly don't know if he ever really forgave me because I ran into him years down the road and the look he had on his face spoke volumes.

If I could have rewound the time, I would never have crossed that line of friendship to date Derrick. Instead, I would have just remained friends because his friendship meant the world to me and so many times I would have given anything to have that friendship back. Once the barrier of friendship is removed and the line is crossed to become more than friends, the assuredness of love and trust must become key factors of communication.

At the time, I should have asked myself these questions: "can I love this person beyond friendship"? If you ever find yourself in this situation, please be honest with your reply to yourself. Also, ask yourself "am I trustworthy"? And include, "Am I willing to allow God to set the precedence for this covenant"? More importantly, "Am I being led by God, or the lust of the flesh"? "Am I enthralled with the mere title of wife"? "Am I willing to yield to a husband and let him lead me"? These should have been the very questions that I should have asked myself before making the decision to marry Derrick.

Seemingly, when the line of friendship to dating is crossed, you can never really get it back when you have a person that may not be willing to totally forgive and put the past behind them. Though I regret hurting Derrick, he could have bailed out a long time before we got married. He had the obligation to return to God and ask God, "FATHER, are you sure this is my covenant wife"? He could have said, "I do not believe there is a mutual agreement, but FATHER, if You say she is the one, is she convicted and convinced of this truth"? "Help her FATHER to know what your will is. Help me FATHER to have wisdom about Thy will."

Today, I have taken responsibility for all I have done, and I fully regret not taking my vows seriously. I regret the hurt and pain that I caused my ex-husband. I can easily blame it on my immaturity at the time but there was no excuse for taking the vows of the LORD and the sacredness of the covenant in vain.

I could not love Derrick the way he deserved to be loved because I didn't love myself. On top of that, I was dealing with low self-esteem issues and so much brokenness on the inside from my past. As friends,

Derrick and I could have prayed about these things and all of my anxieties, and even had patience with the LORD to do a work in me.

Today, I truly thank God who has taken me down a road of restoration, healing and deliverance over the years. I praise God for the person I am today because if it were not for Him, I would still be that awful, wretched, miserable person that I was years ago. I also praise God for bringing me out of a dark place of dealing with low self-esteem and the spirit of rejection. These issues can bring about horrible behaviors and can even hinder you from being able to love yourself and others in a healthy way.

Oftentimes we desire to fall in love, but if we don't love ourselves, we will often bring about misery in that person's life; causing him/her to suffer all because we may be broken on the inside. These days, my self-esteem is in a much healthier place and I can honestly say that I love myself with a healthy dose of love. Now that I've been on a long journey of healing, I can now began to participate in a healthy relationship where I can truly love someone with the willingness to be open, honest and trusting as well as trustworthy.

I can now be a covenant wife because I will be able to determine if my spirit agrees with his spirit. I can ask myself, "What are our commonalities"? "Can he lead me spiritually"? "Can I love him with all of my heart"? These are just a few questions that will allow me to understand if I am being called to enter into a covenant in which I can commit; dedicate; and submit myself without constraints to a person who is sent by God.

I would have loved to encounter Derrick when I grew up spiritually and truly apologized to him of the things I did. I would have asked him to forgive me because of how I hurt him years ago, but he has now passed away. I regret that we never got that chance to really speak again years later. I can only hope that he found it somewhere in his heart to truly forgive me. God blessed him to remarry and hopefully he was able to have the kind of wife he truly deserved.

When we make the lowest of the lowest decisions in our lives, people will tend to turn their backs and give up on us, but God never will. He always remember the covenant that He made with us and He stands by His word when He says He will never leave us, nor will He forsake us. He can take our shame and turn them into life learning lessons. God has spent much time with me over the years; working on me and preparing me for greater days in my life.

As you can see, years ago, I made a horrible mistake in taking the sacredness of the union of marriage for granted, therefore today, I want to encourage others to not make the mistake of taking the sanctity of marriage for granted. Marriage should be taken very seriously. It is a sacred union that should be entered into with careful thought and counseling. I believe the vows should be viewed and understood with careful thought and intentions as well.

The LORD desired that I fully understand the sacredness and sanctity of marriage as well as the seriousness of the covenant that one makes when entering into one of the most sacred unions. Not only have I been forgiven, but He has given me much understanding, wisdom and insight of how sacred a covenant union of marriage is and to not take it lightly.

Not only does the LORD desire that I know about the sanctity of marriage, He desires for all who are considering marriage; as well as those who are already married, to be reminded and to know just how sacred this union truly is and to not take it for granted. If happiness is our only focus, with no willingness of sacrifice, then people will be divorced within 2 years; especially once those honeymoon feelings fade away. Our focus should be much deeper than just the normal reasons of wanting to say "I do".

We have to understand that God's purpose for marriage extends far beyond our own personal happiness and desires. He gave us marriage as a sign of His own eternal and spiritual existence. We should desire to marry for the glory of God and to be a witness of His love; grace; and commitment; even to our children. When the world sees this kind of commitment, now God gets the glory!

Therefore, we must realize how sacred marriage is. It is a covenant that is precious and priceless. The covenant is of all value and should never be viewed as worthless. Marriage is a beautiful and sacred union that should be cherished and protected. For all life is valuable to God and all life is in His hands.

The LORD has helped me to know that out of a sacred union, comes many wonderful blessings. It's what God intended, so if you're deciding to get married, it would be wise to recognize the significance of such a wonderful and sacred union and to prepare as much as you can. We know that no marriage is perfect; it will take much work and dedication; a lot of forgiveness and patience as the two grow together in a union to become even better partners that can last a lifetime!

THE FIRST MARRIAGE

To be the first of anything is very special all in itself. The first marriage occurred in the Garden of Eden. Though the ceremony of the first marriage is not thoroughly described in the Book of Genesis, the union of Adam and Eve did happen. It was an approved union by the Almighty Creator, Himself. Many people question why the first wedding ceremony is not described verbatim; however, there is supporting evidence that is appropriately identified through the story of Adam and Eve, that they were married.

Before Eve came along, Adam was able to explore and learn all about God's beautiful creation of the earth. While living the single life, Adam enjoyed his fellowship time with the One who created him. Throughout this covenant relationship with God, Adam gained much insight and knowledge. He had understanding of the agreement between him and his Creator about how life would be, in living in the Garden of Eden. He was even warned about the tree of the knowledge of good and evil.

Adam was a person created in God's image, so ponder this; Adam had power because God gave it to him. He had the power of intelligence, obedience, and sustenance. Adam was able to name every animal distinctively based on how they would be classified: amphibians; birds; sea life; mammals; and reptiles. He understood his power of obedience, which is why God gave him a commandment.

During this time, Adam could reflect on all that God had done and how He had blessed him. All of the animals that God had created came in pairs. There was male and female of each animal, but Adam didn't have a female companion. God knew that something was missing from Adam's life; a mate! *"And the Lord God said, it is not good that man should be alone; I will make him an help meet for him"* Genesis 2:18 (KJV).

God, in His infinite wisdom knew Adam would need a help mate, so God caused Adam to enter into a deep sleep while He performed the first surgery ever and took a rib from his side and made Eve. God took from Adam's bones and flesh and made a woman. God built Eve physically and mentally to be the perfect companion for Adam. She was to be cherished and valued as being more precious than any natural resource that could be known unto man. And because God made Eve from one of Adam's rib, you can see why the bond was so great between Adam and Eve.

This was truly a significant point in Adam's life and he knew it because his first recorded words regarding Eve were, *"This is now bone of my bones and flesh of my flesh; and she shall be called Woman because she was taken out of Man"* Genesis 2:23 (KJV). So Adam was thrilled at the idea of having a companion, and just like the other living creatures had their very own mate, he now had his own mate. Adam recognized this connection to her because she was surely apart of him and he was a part of her.

God brought Eve to Adam and God initiated the very first marriage in the Garden of Eden. This powerful union helps us to see God's plan for man and woman, coming together in a sacred union (covenant) with God. Not only did God perform the ceremony but He blessed it; He blessed Adam and Eve. This tells us that marriage is a good thing. It's one of the many blessings that God has given us from the beginning.

Though Adam did not find a wife, he identified the role of a man as a husband and that of the woman as a wife. When God brought Eve to Adam and the union was made, this allowed us to see God's plan for man and woman in regards to being united in Holy Matrimony which again, is the covenant God established amongst the two.

Eve was provided in a spiritual context. When God provided Eve as a help mate, she was given as a gift. According to James 1:17 (KJV) *"Every good gift and every perfect gift is from above, and cometh down from the Father of lights, with whom is no variableness, neither shadow of turning."* God already knew Eve was weaker than Adam, but Adam and Eve were symbolic to Christ and the Church. When you think of giving someone a gift, is not the focus of that gift based upon the needs of the person you are giving it too?

Christ was given unto mankind as a gift of Eternal life. Though He was sent into a world with people that are weak; downtrodden; lovers of themselves; and filled with the nature of sin, He, being the gift of life laid down His life for everyone. Think about the love Christ has for the believers that have received Him as a gift. He says in John 10:29 (KJV) "My *Father, which gave them me, is greater than all; and no man is able to pluck them out of my Father's hand"*.

Adam had taken the same stance. Eve was a gift from God, regardless of her falling short of God's glory. Adam stood with her, instead of giving up on her. He did not want Eve to be lost because he loved his God given gift. What exactly is Adam stating about cleaving? Adam is stating that a man shall accept, embrace, guide, lead, love, protect and provide for his spouse along with many other responsibilities including losing his life for her.

In my past marriage, and many marriages of today, sadly grace is not given when one falls short of their promised vows. Regardless of his findings about me, my ex-husband should have remembered his vows to promise to love for better or worse. Once my indiscretions were discovered, that was his moment to decide that he would stand by me and seek God on how to better handle the issues that we had now encountered within our marriage. The marriage of Adam and Eve helps me to understand that the love that Adam had for Eve in knowing that although Eve fell short, and ultimately caused him to do the same, Adam knew he had to stand by her side and accept the consequences for both of their actions.

How do we know that Adam loved Eve? God transformed Adam from clay into a living soul. He did so by breathing into him the breath of life. When God transformed Adam into a living creature, He brought to life Adam's soul. Adam's spirit being given life by God shows that he was able to love Eve, because God is love. We are also given the Spirit of Life when we are in Christ Jesus and Him, being within us.

Since Adam and Eve were blessed to experience the first marriage ever, it is important to know that they were the unique couple. They did not have a wedding party, because they were constantly rejoicing about the goodness of God, nor did they have to pray about or even guess if they were right for one another. They knew they trusted God and in trusting God, they knew they were perfectly made for each other.

Their marriage was really special. For Adam and Eve to have been the first people to be created on the earth, they didn't have a model before them of what a marriage should be. They only had the guiding of a loving FATHER to lead them in their roles of what a husband and wife should be, and this leads to another interesting point; Adam and Eve did not have wedding vows, yet they had a covenant ordained by God.

The marriage between Adam and Eve reflects several facts. 1) He has a relationship with Eve. 2) He has received Eve as a gift to resolve loneliness. 3) She is an added value to his life in which he would not exercise dominion over her; God stipulates she is a help meet for Adam. 4) They will have a family and most importantly – she is his wife and the two shall be one.

The First Marriage

Something else to consider is: 1) Adam and Eve were the first couple who never divorced. 2) They were the first couple who experienced a monogamous relationship. This would model before their children the roles of husband and a wife, because the precedence of a wholesome marriage is to be mirrored throughout the family.

God created marriage as a partnership between one man and one woman. A marriage is a beautiful depiction of who God is. 1 John 4:7 (KJV) states *"Beloved, let us love one another: for love is of God; and everyone that loveth is born of God and knoweth God"*. God is love! Marriage resembles God's covenant relationship with His people; a people whom God loves very much. Marriage is the groundwork of His glory being exemplified in all aspects through a beautiful union.

When you consider the prospects of a partnership, it should be encouraging. Think about this; there are some situations that are difficult for one to hurdle over; but when you have someone coaching and encouraging you, the burdened is then lightened. When the two approach a taunting situation, they can collaborate to achieve the best possible outcome.

The partnership between a husband and wife is not to be a clandestine tactic for concealing truths from one another, but the partnership should be the bridge upon which you cross together to defeat any challenges. God will uphold your walking together, and will help you conquer your fears; troubles; and woes.

The integrity of love is founded upon the heart of those who pray unto God with appreciation for their loved one. The pledge of trust allows the peace to remain present and is not obscured by any attempt of the enemy to desecrate their bond. The intricate details of what happens between a husband and wife should not be shared with anyone else. Yet as they walk together because they agree together, they both can go to God in prayer about anything they need answers for. Everyone should be bound by the sanctity of marriage to protect and honor their loved ones.

It is sad when we see that some people do not honor their marriages, families, or their homes. Some people tend to have little regard for the things they are doing outside of the home and how it will affect the home life in the long run. Marriage should be honored amongst all. This includes people on the outside of the marriage; everyone should respect a union.

"Marriage is honorable in all and the bed undefiled: but the whoremongers and adulterers God will judge" Hebrews 13:4 (KJV). Many people assume Hebrews 13:4 implies they can do anything they want pertaining to their marriage bed with no consequence, but that is not so. Examine the verse: this means we will not bring Jack, Jill and everyone else from down the hill into the privacy of our marriage. This means we will not bring pornography or lewd things into our space. Some of the older couples will even tell you that they do not have a television in their bedroom.

Defiling the marriage bed has much to do about the mindset as well as activities of the body. The marriage bed is not defiled as long as it's just the two of you in that bed. Don't even bring other people issues into your sacred space. Most of all if you have done anything that could negate your spouse's love for you, you can repent and turn away from it. Yield unto the LORD and pray for the purification of your marriage to abound beyond any misfortune, mistakes, and misunderstandings.

Deciding to get married is a big step in any relationship. Once the decision has been made to get married, you both should discuss how you got to the point of that decision, and walk in the agreement of that decision. Be sure to discuss boundaries, limitations, and rules. For instance, whomever is a friend to one – should be a friend to both. This does not mean the best friend of a man must be a best friend of the wife. What is implied here is that a friend of either should have a mutual respect of one and the other; and be willing to honor and be trustworthy.

This means the friend does not get the opportunity to cause confusion; lead into temptation, or have corruptible behaviors. Psalms 1:1 (KJV) states, *"Blessed is the man that walketh not in the counsel of the ungodly, nor standeth in the way of sinners, nor sitteth in the seat of the scornful"*. Rules must be established, and if you need help with establishing the rules, seek God and be open to His Spirit for instructions in righteous living.

We often hear of people having prenuptials involved in their marriage contract, but there shouldn't even be any prenuptial agreements because that implies there is a way out before the couple actually begin their service unto one another. Yes, serve as a help meet; serve for sacrifice; serve with a deep-rooted desire to be charitable and compassionate toward your spouse. This will permit the opportunity to persevere for all things that are best needed for the union.

Be sure that the one you decide to live your life with grasp your beliefs, morals, and values. That way when you begin your life as one, you start on the same page. When the story is revealed to your children of how you met, it should be a memory of joy. Years down the road, when discussions of how you two disagreed for the first time come up – it should be described with laughter because as you look back at it, you overcame the situations and circumstances.

We should be able to look upon the union of Adam and Eve and see just how special their marriage truly was and to see the love sacrifice that Adam made in choosing to stay with Eve, and ultimately take part in suffering with her. Being determined to reach the pinnacle of their love; achieving their goals and identifying their weaknesses without giving up; is what couples should be striving for today. Longsuffering should be a catalyst to help them attain success within their marriage.

God's plan for each marriage, is that each partner will grow and prosper and become a powerful union that God's glory can be revealed through.

Marriage is not only vows of promise, it is the ability to look beyond one's faults and love them from a place of where you want to be loved. Encourage your spouse; motivate them; and love them. The pinnacle of love is trust, therefore you should be able to trust one another when deciding to enter into such a life-long commitment of love.

THE SACRED VOWS

At the beginning of the book, I shared how I took my marriage for granted in not honoring my sacred union and vows. As I took my vows during my wedding ceremony, I did not have the decency to take into consideration of what each vow really meant and therefore it felt far too easy for me to dishonor them. Through my relationship with the LORD, He has helped me to have a much better and healthy understanding of those sacred vows. My prayer is for those who are considering marriage to take a closer look at the marital vows and get a better understanding; with careful thought and intentions of what you will be committing to.

When people get married, they require witnesses. When they enter into a promise with one another, people will be there to bear witness of that agreement: that the bride and groom will be joined together in holy matrimony; but it must be understood that God is the primary witness. Less than often will the people who witnessed your nuptials come and state, "Oh no, you shall not divorce because you took an oath by promise and said for better or worse." We sometimes unfortunately, do not hear those voices that want to hold us accountable to what they witnessed at the marriage ceremony. If people would take into consideration that the LORD God Himself is a part of this union, would they then make a greater effort to be sustained in their marriages?

Please take your word as being one of the most precious gems in this world to offer and give unto someone else, because your word defines the very essence of your being. A person who keeps their word is a person to be honored. For this reason, we honor God, because He always keeps His promises. Let's take a look at the marriage vows that are normally made on the day of a wedding ceremony:

"I……take you……. To be my wife/husband. To have and to hold from this day forward, for better, for worse, for richer, for poorer; in sickness and in health; to love and to cherish; till death do us part, according to God's holy law; and this is my solemn vow."

These are the vows that we have taken part of at some point in our lives or either we know someone close to us who have. When we get married, we are giving our word; as a sacred promise before the LORD, that we will keep our promises to God and to one another. These vows should be our way of consecrating our relationship before the LORD, because they are sacred to God. Let's take a closer look at each one of the sacred vows.

- <u>I take you to be my wife.</u> When a man takes a woman to be his wife, he has accepted her and is committing to spend the rest of his life with her. He is making a commitment unto her that he will love her as Christ loves the church and gave His life for her (Ephesians 5:25).

  Gentlemen, your role as a husband is more than just committing to remain with your spouse until death do you part. You are also making an oath to stand by your wife; to support her, and substantiate her. You are vowing to teach her in the ways of the LORD. Your duty and responsibility are first unto God, but you must be accountable unto her as well.

You must believe in her and the potential she has in which to become a great wife. You will also need to help her to be a superb mother to your children. You should be able to aid her when she lacks the ability to stand for the faith that you two will now walk in as one.

You are the leader and therefore must be able to keep the alignment in the family system. You are the patriarch, and the ways you govern the home should be in the will of God. Gentlemen, you are the ones who must make the sacrifices. You cannot afford to be selfish, but with diligence, lead the family in prayer; guide them with truth and obey the Word of God, for in your leading, you will also be a servant unto them.

You are to love your wife as does Christ loves the Church, which to say His bride. Love your spouse in the same like manner. When a man loves his wife, he loves himself. With this notion, the husband profits from this love, as does his wife. Therefore, when some people profess that their spouse complete them, they are not negating the power of God to complete, deliver, heal, or validate them in their entirety, but rather they come to understand God can use the spouse to help them in the areas where they lack joy, peace, knowledge, and wisdom.

- <u>I take you to be my husband.</u> When a woman takes a man to be her husband, she has accepted him and is willing to commit to spend the rest of her life with him. She is coming into agreement to be one with him. She is coming into submission to her husband as she does unto the LORD (Ephesians 5:22).

Ladies, are you ready to say, "Yes, I want to be a good wife"? Here is something you must consider. Your spouse will love you in the respect he has for women. If your spouse had no respect for his own mother, more than likely he will not respect you. In the same regards, did you respect your dad? Did your dad exemplify the duties of a husband before you with your mother? Did your dad model a relationship between himself and God? These questions are very important to understand. Did you have a broken relationship with your dad? If you can identify with any of these questions and you are planning to become married, please pray sincerely:

> Dear Holy Father, Please, allow Your Holy Spirit to help me with my infirmities, for I am to be a wife. I so hope my husband finds me worthy to be united with him as one. Therefore, because I did not have an earthly dad to model how I am to be treated by a man, can you allow Your Holy Spirit to help me? Will Your Holy Spirit intercede for me when I think I should be possessive, or when I am faced with insecurities about my husband? Since I never saw the faithfulness of a man – Will You, please help me to see Your faithfulness exemplified through my husband? Will You increase my ability to trust in You, so that I will be able to love my husband with patience? Will You, Holy Father help him to be worthy of my submission unto him that he will show me appreciation? As I become one with my husband; will You, Father help us to love one another in the capacity in which You ordained, without the lust of the flesh; lust of the eyes, and the pride of life. I do love him, but I love You Abba, in spirit and in truth. Will You therefore, bless our union? In Jesus Christ I pray Amen.

Ladies, you have a load to carry when becoming a wife. Whatever, your rearing was, you must allow the man to lead and be your head. You must be willing to pray for his strength and be willing to obey him as he leads you by way of the Word of God. You must be able to walk equally as a help mate, and not as an officer for his justice. With diligence, you are to serve him in a way in which he honors the Word of God; that he has found a good thing. Do not listen to naysayers, but love and respect your husband and also pray for your husband.

- <u>To have and to hold.</u> To have someone is to receive or accept the total self of that individual. It's not ownership, but rather a promise of unconditional acceptance. To hold someone is a form of physical affection and is like making a vow to be available to the other individual, while promising to cherish, value, and protect them; such as a prized treasure.

To have a person is to have and accept all of them. Not part of them, but all of them. It's so easy to make these vows at the beginning because we are so excited about spending our lives with one another but later on in the years, it may not be as easy as it once was to give your total self to your partner, but be encouraged to try.

A promise to make ourselves readily available to the other partner goes a long way. For instance, the giving of our time to our spouse may sometimes pose an issue if our schedules are ridiculously full. Also, if we have many chores and obligations to attend to, this can often leave us with less time for our partners. But here is the opportunity to refocus on our priorities. If you both are employed and are working different hours (or whatever the distraction may be) the first thing you want to do is plan a time to pray together.

Praying together is the adhesion you will need to hold your marriage together. As you both grow in the LORD together, to become one with each other, you both will see God at work. If you desire to, you both can pray that you have the same work hours and God will do it. His Word will not return to Him void, and since God ordained Adam to be a husband and Eve his wife, when Adam spoke, he did so by the authority of God. Adam said the two will become one. In your prayer time with one another, pray like this:

> Dear Holy Father, We believe on one accord that Your Word is a light unto our path. We so desire to honor Your Word and walk as one in spirit, but FATHER, we both work different schedules. FATHER, we need to have more personal time with each other. FATHER, if it is your will that You will fix it, we pray that we work the same schedules; or if it be Thy will Holy God, that my husband becomes promoted in order that I devote more time to the home, can You fix it according to Your will. Nonetheless, if we both must be employed, allow Your Holy Spirit to help us to be content with all things. Help us still to serve You in spirit and in truth and to do what honors You – to wait on You and have Your will be done in our life. Let there be no backlash or retaliation to this request that we submit, asking Christ to mediate on our behalf. In Jesus Christ we pray as we abide in Him as one, Amen.

Regardless of what the obstacle is, you must be able to identify anything that hinders the time spent with one another. Neglecting your time with each other can make your partner feel less important. The impact can begin to open doors for mischief, which may result in issues within your marriage. If you have the time to embrace each other, your time together will allow you to respect one another's responsibilities.

You could possibly even find yourself guilty of not desiring to be sexually intimate with your mate as much as you once were for whatever reason. It could be because you find yourself being tired all the time and if this be the case, ask your partner to help out more with the workload so that you can get the proper rest you need. When you are well rested, you will find that you have more energy for your partner.

If you have found yourself guilty of losing interest in wanting to be intimate with your partner, now is the time to remember your vows. Once you get married, you must remember that your body do not belong to just you anymore. You are now one together. You now have an obligation to be available for your spouse as you vowed to be. Now if you are truly tired or not feeling well, then your partner should be more understanding but if you're using excuses not to be there for your partner in the way they desire, then you must re-examine your motives, along with your vows.

We again must validate our oath; we said to have and to hold, meaning we will embrace and engage our minds with one another. Here again is an opportunity to pray that we have our priorities in order. We do not want to find ourselves not having time for one another, because you'll eventually not have the time to pursue God together in prayer and studying His Word. If you forsake the unity of coming together in the presence of God – it is possible to open yourself to an ungodly entity.

Our time cannot always belong to everybody else and not to our spouse. You should place God first; family second; and business and everyone else third. That is a very healthy order for all of our lives. Prioritizing our schedules can be beneficial to understanding the needs of one another as well.

- <u>For better.</u> If things are really good within your marriage, it is considered to be effective or of great quality; meaning that all things are well. People are happy to commit to an individual for better, knowing all is well with them and that there are great days ahead to be shared with one another. It's also a great blessing to be with someone who understands that growing and maturing is a natural part of life and welcomes it. Are we examining the obvious? You can see what is evident in each other's lives and what brings about joy and peace. You cannot be selfish to withhold anything that will continue in their bliss, therefore, try to be supportive of those things. If you can be the producer, you should be willing to assume that responsibility.

- <u>For worse.</u> If things are bad or get worse in a marriage, it is considered to be of poor quality or less good or desirable. Can you persevere with your partner when their personal problems have taken a turn for the worse? Can you still maintain hope when your partner is going through some rough trials in his/her life? Being with someone for worse, doesn't mean we bail out on them at the sign of trouble or when they are going through some of the worst times of their lives.

Remember, this is a 3-person relationship, so do not forget that God is nigh. He is observing all things and will bring them into a more distinctive perspective for you. James 4:6-8 (KJV) states, *"But He giveth more grace. Wherefore He saith, God resisteth the proud, but giveth grace unto the humble. Submit yourselves therefore to God. Resist the devil, and he will flee from you. Draw nigh to God, and He will draw nigh to you. Cleanse your hands, ye sinners; and purify your hearts, ye double minded."*

Therefore, be willing to go before God and pray for your spouse and not against your spouse. You must be relentless and willing to lament for them. Lamenting is a deeper cry – it is petitioning God from the depth of your soul about something. You should be willing to go before God on your face to request God's help in any matter regarding your spouse.

The Song of Solomon 2:16 (KJV) states, *"My beloved is mine, and I am his"*. The statement, "my beloved" denotes the assurance that you both are engrafted into this marriage as one. This means you adore, cherish, and are willing to honor your dedication to one another. You are not in this covenant relationship alone. You both have one another to talk with about your issues, but more so, you both have God to lead and direct your course on this journey of marriage.

If for some reason things began to take a turn for the worse regarding your spouse's attitude or bad habits, and the individual is not willing to yield unto God's ways or even counseling, then there are other things to be considered. People have to desire to change and get better, not only for themselves but for their family.

If that individual know that they have a problem in a particular area of their lives, and they take on an attitude of not wanting to address the issue, this can tend to create issues of an entirely different nature. If you have issues, identify them, and talk with your spouse about them. Do not ignore them and take on an "I don't care" attitude, because you are no longer a single individual and what you do, not only affects you but it affects the one that you're married to, therefore your bad habits and attitude can no longer be ignored. If you say you love your spouse, then you should want to own up to your faults and seek to do better.

For example, if your spouse gets involved in an affair with someone, the person whom the spouse is involved with could become a jealous lover and that person may want to bring harm to you. It is understood when you endure much pain, there is also degradation, but shall you be punished because of your spouse's infidelity? NO!!! There are some behaviors that God is simply not pleased with. We are instructed in 2 Timothy 2:22 (KJV) *"Flee also youthful lusts: but follow righteousness, faith, charity, peace, with them that call on the Lord out of a pure heart."*

It is important to note that if a spouse is abusing their partner, or is sleeping around and putting their life in danger with STD's, these are major red flags that cannot be ignored. If your spouse is posing a threat to your health and to the livelihood of you and your family, you have to know when it's time to go. When we say that we will marry for worse, you better know what that can sometimes intel. If a person is experiencing domestic abuse, you must seek help immediately! This means that an evil spirit has entered into your partner and now seeks to mistreat, abuse, and destroy you. Abuse is not just physical; it can be mental, verbal, and emotional, as well as financial and sexual. If your partner has started to abuse you and gotten to a place where your life is being threatened, understand that it's not going to stop. If that individual doesn't recognize that they have a problem and desire to seek help, you have to take it upon yourself to remove yourself from that toxic relationship. There are ways that you can exit safely, so if you find yourself in this situation, seek help immediately!

God does not have us to stay within bad marriages where we are being abused; flat out disrespected; or even where the spouse refuse to get help. Never let someone convince you that it's healthy to stay within a broken marriage where the individual is getting worse and worse; refusing help; and is putting your life in danger. Don't be foolish. You have to know when to stay and know when it's time to go.

You are not being directed to evaluate your belief, faith and hope in your spouse. If you are truly believing God – you must place your spouse before that spiritual text and determine if their qualities resemble that of Christ. If a wayward spouse is willing to repent before the LORD; receive help and counseling; and be willing to change their habits, the marriage can be worth salvaging. After all, forgiveness is another gem of love that you can give to your spouse, but with forgiveness comes much work that one must be willing to commit to in order to turn things around in the marriage.

- <u>For richer.</u> If you are wealthy, you are considered to have a great deal of money or assets. We certainly don't mind committing ourselves to someone who was either already wealthy or who became wealthy along the way. We don't normally find any issues with that. When someone has a great deal of wealth, that's always a plus to the relationship which will most likely bring good times and allow you to fully provide for your family and daily needs, but wealth should not determine who we are to love or not love.

- <u>For poorer.</u> You could be lacking in sufficient money to be able to live at a standard that is considered comfortable or normal. If you went into a marriage where there was wealth, vowing to stay with someone for poorer can certainly come to test the heart and the true intentions of a person. If your spouse was once wealthy and lost it all, you must remember the vows you made with that individual. If your intentions were true in the beginning, you should still be able to love and cherish that individual the same way you did when they had plenty of wealth.

Money, nor health should never be the reason to make you question if you want to remain married to an individual. Situations and circumstances can change from time to time within a marriage but your vows to that individual should never be a question if they all of a sudden lost everything they had. Real love is what holds you together – not money or the lack of. To vow to be with someone for poorer, is saying that no amount of money, or the shortage thereof will affect the love that you have for the individual and not only is that real talk, but that's real love.

- <u>In sickness.</u> When you are sick, you can be affected physically or mentally. You can also be affected with disease or ill health. It is simple and quite easy to make vows when an individual is currently in good health, but what if ten years down the road an accident happens and now your spouse have now become reliable for you to take care of them?

Sometimes our fears of not understanding the outcome of a situation hinders our ability to focus on the needs of another. Matthew 7:12 (KJV) explains, *"Therefore all things whatsoever ye would that men should do to you, do ye even so to them"*. If you were needing someone to care for you, should you not be willing to care for that person? Remember, love is reciprocity. You must be willing to do for your spouse as you expect your spouse to do for you. Though, we don't ever want to imagine our partner being in a state of helplessness, however, are you willing to be strong and try to remain loyal and committed to the one whom you made vows with? This is hardly ever thought about when considering going into marriage but there have been instances where one partner no longer wanted to be in the marriage because their spouse took sick and was constantly needing medical care.

It is unfair to the spouse to just take up and leave the marriage because they are no longer in the state they were in when you got married. To vow to be with someone in sickness means that you are vowing to be there for them and help take care of them no matter what may come. A physical ailment should not cause us to lose the love we have for someone.

It may not be easy, but if situations like this occur, we should not bolt on our spouses, but pray and ask the LORD for help to keep you strong for your partner in every way that they need you. People may take sick but your vows must come into remembrance when taking care of your loved ones.

God forbids something happens to your spouse and you find yourself struggling with wanting to be there for them; just know that you are human and you're not a bad person. It happens to many people, but you can call on the LORD, who's your ever present Help and He will strengthen you and help you to be there for your spouse in a way where you can still express your love in taking care of them.

- In health. When you are healthy, you are free from illness or injury; you are sound in body and mind. Committing to someone while they are in good health is not hard to do. Naturally we want our partner to be in good health and hopefully over the years remain in good health. It is good when you and your spouse can encourage each other in taking necessary steps to maintain and ensure good health. After all, we should want to take good care of the temple that the LORD has given us and to be aware to not abuse these bodies by constantly eating bad food or using substances. We should want to maintain good health as long as we can to help provide for our spouse and family.

- <u>To love.</u> When we love someone, we show strong and deep affection for our loved ones. We often display intense feelings towards one another. To love someone or be in love is what often leads us into making marriage vows to one another. When we love someone, we tend to do all kinds of thoughtful things to make our loved ones feel very special. We think about them all throughout the day; we send them beautiful roses or flowers;

we write them poems and love letters; we cook their favorite meals or take them out to their special events. We even profess our love to them and shower them with all kinds of wonderful gifts.

All of these things are ways that we show our love and affections for one another. We understand that as time moves us along in life, these displays of love and affection can sometimes be far and few in between. As people of flaws, we can tend to move away from doing the very things that once made our spouse feel like they were the most special person in the world.

Not only do we have to remember to keep the flame alive in our marriage, but we have to continue to strive to love our partners as Christ loves us. No matter how long you've been married, try to keep loving your spouse to the best of your ability. 1 Corinthians 13:4-5 (NIV) explains love best, *"Love is patient, love is kind. It does not envy, it does not boast, it is not proud. It does not dishonor others, it is not self-seeking, it is not easily angered, it keeps no record of wrongs"*. We know that no one is perfect. We may even tend to struggle with keeping the affection going within our relationships over time. The feeling of being in love comes and goes but vowing to love someone goes much deeper than just feelings.

Agape love is the highest form of love. It is a deep, and sacrificial kind of love. It is selfless and unconditional. It is the kind of love that God has for mankind. It is the greatest love of all. When I think about agape love, and the covenant relationship between the Church, which is You and I, and our Husband, which is God; I think of how the Bride-which is You and I, are totally cared for, meaning we come to a place where there's nothing missing, and there's nothing broken. God is our Strong Tower; He is our Refuge and Strength; our Protector;

our Divine Healer; our Deliverer; our Provider; our Redeemer, and so much more! He is the total package. The "Husband" is constantly fulfilling His duties in taking care of His beloved "Bride". His love for us is unconditional. He doesn't have one foot in the door and one foot out of the door. He is all in; for better or for worse. He will never leave you, nor will He forsake you. He is the perfect Gentleman.

I think of how God loves us and how patient He is with us. Even though we have many flaws, He display patience in dealing with us. He knows that we won't remain in a broken state forever, but that He is focused on loving us through our many mess ups. We may be a beautiful mess today, but He always see what we can become as we grow in Him.

This is the kind of love that you can strive for and even display throughout your marriage. When we truly learn how to love like this, we can learn to be patient with our spouse's flaws. Our spouse may have immature ways at the beginning of the marriage but we can look down the road to see them becoming a much better version of themselves if we can be patient through the process.

We pray and have hope that they will get better within time. People can even learn how to be kind to one another from time to time and not just deliberately be rude just because they are married to each other. Some people have the notion that just because they have been married for several years that they can just behave badly and that their spouse will just have to deal with how they are. This is not a healthy mindset to develop.

Never get comfortable in your bad habits. We can grieve the Holy Spirit in how we treat one another. The scriptures says that *"He who finds a wife finds a good thing and receives favor from the Lord"* Proverbs 18:22 (NIV). For example, if a husband has a flourishing business but he constantly mistreats his wife, he may began to lose favor with the LORD. His business may began to suffer and other things may even began to spiral downhill within his life. We have to be mindful of how we treat one another because the LORD sees all that we do. I believe that if you want to be successful in whatever you do in life, remember to treat your spouse well and things will go well with you in the LORD.

To envy your spouse, is to be jealous of what blessings and gifts they have; what they are experiencing in great seasons of their lives; and who they are or have become. Your spouse is the one that is closest to you other than God. Your spouse should be the very one cheering you on when you have gotten a promotion; started a business; written a book, etc. Envy can tear a marriage apart. When we really love someone, we will know that envy has no place our marriage or relationships.

To love your spouse is to love yourself. After all, you are to become as one person, so express your love one to another. Take the time daily to say "I love you" because you should not assume your spouse knows how much you love them. If you have the indwelling of the Holy Spirit, you should find it easy to exemplify the Fruit of the Spirit as are found in Galatians 5:22-23 (KJV), " 22) *But the fruit of the Spirit is love, joy, peace, longsuffering, gentleness, goodness, faith, 23) Meekness, temperance: against such there is no law."* The Fruit of the Spirit is your bonding material in your covenant relationship.

- <u>To cherish.</u> When we cherish one another, we want to hold each other dear, and we want to protect and care for each other lovingly. At the beginning of a relationship, it is so easy to cherish one another but this act should be followed throughout the years. If the cherished feelings you once had for your spouse begins to leave during the course of the marriage, have faith in knowing that God can bring those feelings back.

God can restore your love for your spouse. Recall that Christ has said, where your treasure is, there is also the matter of your heart Matthew 6:21. When you cherish your spouse, you will acknowledge their efforts. When you appreciate the smallest of their tasks to appease you – you will show them how you have honor for them. When you demonstrate gratitude for their value, you can reveal your gratefulness of their worth. Your love matters and how you exemplify it, is very important.

Some people tend to think that if they don't always feel that vitality, then their love is dissipating, but that is not always the case. You must determine if your routine is not providing you with the excitement, you initially experienced. This is normal, but you can explore new things that can rejuvenate the life of your marriage. Real love never dies because love is symbolic of life, so remember this in the distance of the race you are running. Don't ever give up on having loving feelings for your spouse because the more you keep God at the center of your marriage and have faith that things will get better, they will. Make the decision that you're in it for the long haul and that you will tough it out until the loving feelings return that make you want to cherish your spouse as you once did in the courting phase of your relationship.

- <u>Till death do we part.</u> If a person is dying, they are facing the end of life. Marriages should last until death takes place of either partner. We know that we are beings of many flaws and so many things can happen throughout the course of a marriage that may make it impossible to stay together for the sake of the marriage. The scripture says, *"Therefore what God has joined together, let no one separate"* Mark 10:9 (NIV). Death should be the only thing that separates us from marriage. The intent should be to stay together and come what may, our attitudes towards one another should be the desire of the promise to work things out. In every way that you can, try to work things out.

Sadly, we know that there are some conditions where a marriage may have to end due to people's hearts being hardened towards one another; people being unwilling to change and deliberately causing pain to others; being unequally yoked; adulteries; putting someone's lives in danger; and so on.

Marriage is a lifelong commitment, and I now understand why we should not enter into it lightly. Years ago, I took this meaning for granted, but thanks be to God, I understand the seriousness of this union today. Marriage, as God intended it, is a commitment for life – during good and not so good times.

When the tough gets going in our marriages, it's easy to want to run to divorce court. Try not to take the easy way out, but try to do what may feel like the hard thing to do – which is to try and stay together and work things out if things are able to be worked out that is.

Our vows exemplify the meaning of our hearts. We are delicate when placing our trust in the hands of others, yet, we are pleased when someone accepts us for who we are. Marriage is a beautiful institution that should not be taken lightly, but we must always be willing to pray and ponder the will of God.

If we are so led by His Spirit that He has answered our prayers, so then always let His will be done. Once again, never take for granted the life of another, if you are not going to be committed; dedicated; or a keeper of your promises, avoid any misleading to the altar. Be sure that you are ready to stand before God and your witnesses to keep your word, and take notice and careful thought of the sacred vows that you are planning to commit to.

AFTER A WEDDING COMES A MARRIAGE

Oftentimes we dream and prepare for one of the biggest moments of our lives, and for many, that is falling in love and getting married. Once we have met that special one and fallen in love, all seems right with the world! Before we realize it, our minds began racing towards planning all of the intricate details of a wedding.

Oftentimes we put so much focus on the wedding itself: the preparations; the dress; the ring; the guy; the girl; the honeymoon; the decorations and so on. The whole set up of a wedding is great in itself but all of that pales in comparison of what it takes to commit to the longevity of a marriage.

So now, your dream day has arrived, and you are now gathered with your family and friends and is preparing to say your sacred vows to the love of your life! Your bridesmaids look adorable in the beautiful color you have chosen for them. The groomsmen look dashing in their tuxedos. The sanctuary is adorned with roses and flowers; accentuating the beautiful bride in her wedding gown. The guests are present and accounted for.

As you both are now standing at the altar, preparing to say "I do", you will now make the promise to love and cherish each other for the rest of your lives. There is no doubt in your minds that there is anything that could hinder either of you, and there is no procrastination. Both of you are ready and filled with bliss. As the Pastor officiates the ceremony, you are overwhelmed with joy at the thought of starting your life with your forever partner. And so now you both are pronounced as husband and wife, and from there, the lifetime journey begins! From that moment of introduction as Mr. and Mrs., you both are ready to aim for your combined goals; defeat the challenges ahead; and define your powers. How Breathtaking!

After you both have enjoyed one of the most wonderful and special events of your lives, the next day you have now awakened to a new reality of having to live out your lives with the person that you said your vows to and oh, what a reality to wake up to! The reality of now being married, reveals all possibilities and probabilities to come. You start this married life with a readiness to become selfless and a willingness to sacrifice for the one which you chose to love as a spouse. No longer can you afford to have selfish thinking and to only be concerned about your own individual needs, but now you must assess the entire needs of another person.

With changing your positions in life, you have accepted the charge with all diligence to be dependable, loyal, and reliable unto someone else. Because of the decision to enter into an agreement of commitment; dedication, and service, you should be enthusiastic about your obligation to the involvement with your spouse. You have a newfound respect for the accountability to care for, honor, love and protect, the vows that you made to one another, because you made those vows in the presence of a loving and gracious God. It is His intent for marriage to be considered as another facet of His glory to be shown in all the earth through such a powerful union; therefore, you need to take good care of one another and to handle with care, the precious gift that God gave to you.

Once you have embarked onto this new reality, you embrace the adjustments that are now required to make. For instance, you need to allow for adequate space. You will have to become adjusted to living and sharing the same space with someone in a home. It can be a little challenging when getting used to the day-to-day habits of another person.

Sometimes, people do not consider how important the function of space is. For instance, space is not just an area within a room, or setting up our personal belongings, but being considerate of allowing space for your spouse to ponder their thoughts. Once you establish the appropriate space, you must consider the other person's habits. This may seem minor in the beginning, but if you are not use to people sharing your space, then you need to have some serious discussions.

You can find that some people's habits can be very annoying; frustrating, and even difficult to adjust to at times, but that's a good time to remember just how loving and patient your heavenly FATHER is when it comes to you. We all have different ways of thinking and doing things so it may not always be easy to adjust to at first. A very important scripture to focus upon is 1 Corinthians 13:4-7 (KJV); "4) *Charity suffereth long, and is kind; charity envieth not; charity vaunteth not itself, is not puffed up, 5) Doth not behave itself unseemly, seeketh not her own, is not easily provoked, thinketh no evil; 6) Rejoiceth not in iniquity, but rejoiceth in the truth; 7) Beareth all things, believeth all things, hopeth all things, endureth all things.*"

As we examine this powerful text, we should understand that charity denotes love, which indicates love is not to be switched on for convenience, because love can last forever. The gentleness of love signifies there is much respect in loving someone. This scripture tells us that love does not envy, which suggest there is no greediness, or resentment involved, but acceptance and gratitude. When we look at the aspect of love not being a matter to vaunt itself; that would mean your deeds do not have to be bragged about but rather, makes it easier for your spouse to appreciate all of your efforts. Nor will you find that love is proud but rather endured with your ability to be humble.

Your response in love is to be able to forgive, and not dwell on the faults of your loved one, therefore you will not find yourself easy to be provoked. In this case, my ex-husband constantly dwelt on my indiscretion that I made the day before my wedding. He couldn't seem to get past it, nor could he bring himself to forgive me to the point of working things out.

If you find yourself being challenged in your marriage, try to respond with forgiveness, and you will not find yourself plotting to deprive the other person. You will be elated about the good of resolving matters with the truth; for love escalates you beyond the place of subtle reactions to a place of mutual agreement and understandings.

The above scriptures are also best to keep in mind as you start your new life together. Each verse can help guide you through some of the growing pains of your marriage. It is important to take the time to realize that there is now two different households coming together and two different ways of how you both were raised.

Did you both come out of a healthy environment, or were there some dynamics that caused long enduring pain? Were you and your spouse taught how to share, or were you reared in a selfish place? Did you always play the rescuer in the family or were you the one who was to blame? Did you compete for attention, or were you content with being isolated? Were you both reared in love, patience, and sacrifice? Were either of you recognized or rewarded for accomplishments and achievements?

These are just a few questions to consider and that is why 1 Corinthians 13:4-7 can be the bridge over your troubles to help you meet one another in a place of peace. You must consider that there are now two different mindsets and a whole lot of in between. There's much to be adjusted and more to adjust to, because while you are trying to relinquish the power of just your own, you are making joint efforts, and joint plans to help you both grow into a special place of unity.

These are just the pains and joys of working through getting to know each other better and also learning to accept one another on a whole other level. You can learn to give grace and space to one another as you grow and learn the differences that make up who you are.

Since we are all unique in our own way and because there is no one else in the earth like us, we must identify with those things that are great and not so great about us. We can always work on our weaknesses to become better people and better partners but the key thing here is to be willing to change and come up higher in our thinking. Otherwise we will stunt our growth and make life hard with our partners.

As you both transition from being single to being married, more of your true nature will unfold. Some of the behaviors that your spouse have may even astound you, and some noticeable patterns that your spouse display will confirm your curiosities. In addition, a spouse may have bad manners which are unbelievable, but nonetheless, for better or worse you bring yourself into a place of acceptance.

This is the time when you will learn the contents of your own heart. Realizing that you and your spouse are different can be a wonderful thing because you both must learn how to bring balance to any indifferences that the two of you may have. The blending is not so difficult; it is the terms of your agreement that you may find most challenging.

Your vows are the verbal contract, and you should not violate the oral bond. Once you both move into the same dwelling, you will then see that there are more differences than similarities and that is okay if you both learn how to compromise and respect one another's values and morals. Once again, it's like bringing in two totally different households and merging them into one. There are two different up-bringing's; two different viewpoints/mentalities; two different maturity levels; different habits; and two different pasts are now all coming together under one roof! Whew! It does sound a little scary, but that's reality.

Sometimes, though unfortunate, we do not see the hidden, alarming natures until long after we have said our "I do's." "I do" statements are those that show we are willing to conform, but what about the statements that indicate a reluctance to sacrifice and submit? For instance, before we get married there are things that we reveal about ourselves to one another and rarely will someone tell their proposed spouse "I do not want to clean up the house." That certainly would be a red flag but just imagine if the "I don't…." scenarios were the topic of discussion during your engagement. Would that not offer an avenue of deeper conversations? It would divulge information that either person can accept or reject.

If these types of discussions occurred prior to getting married, then there would be less surprises because you were informed of your spouse's habits and behavior patterns beforehand. There are arguments that can escalate when a person does not clean up after himself/herself, or one who does not cook, or even that does not contribute to helping more and doing more around the house. It is baffling that so many people do not have those discussions before they get married, but it is helpful so that you don't feel blind-sighted beforehand.

We all have viewpoints of what we believe the man's role should be as well as the woman's role in the home. Today's society lead people to think of the man's role to only get up and go to work and come home at the end of the day, and kick back as he watches television; awaiting his wife to cook him dinner. He may even play with the kids a bit before going to bed.

On the other hand, we tend to visualize the woman's role as stay at home mothers, yet she has a responsibility to maintain the home, such as cleaning and organizing. She sets the atmosphere in the dwelling as a peaceful space. Her duties may often extend beyond the boundaries of the home, such as going to PTA meetings or after school basketball practice. She then comes home and start dinner, while helping the kids with their homework and after dinner, she may now bathe the children, clean up after everyone, and lastly, try to find time with her husband before going to bed.

The two above scenarios would be idea based on the plan you made with one another before you became married. The wife oftentimes tend to have more of a workload in the marriage. Husbands, please don't get comfortable in just thinking its ok for your wife to do the majority in the home. If you are able to learn how to cook and clean and do other chores from time to time, you won't find yourself being lost if your wife were to take sick or become where she isn't able to do for the home as much. It would make good practice to learn how to assist in other areas of the home to be of help to your wife and children.

Discussions are so vital to setting up your own practices and routines for your family life, but unintentionally, people may bring in habits from the experiences of their parents. Many people have grown up in homes where the above example was the order that were displayed before them. Such patterns may now be incorporated into their own households. If the husband never picked up after himself while growing up, and was never taught to do so; he must learn the responsibility of doing these things. The more husbands are mindful of being able to assist their wives with certain duties, the more it can help to lessen arguments between the two.

If no understanding comes to such things, then poor habits can come into practice within the household. We tend to bring certain habits and mindsets into the relationship that we are now building with our significant other. If the husband grew up in a single parent home and never had a father figure around, he may struggle with guiding, loving and teaching his own children.

A wife who had no desire to learn how to cook or never learned how to clean her home will find it a challenge with doing these chores in her own household. She may have even grown up in a household where her mother didn't work and her father mainly supported the home. She may not feel that it's necessary that she should work, and if that be the case, then these are the important discussions to have before getting married. It is a good thing to be on the same page with your spouse so that no one feels blind-sighted upon entering into wedded bliss!

So view it this way, if you must live as one, then you must be able to see one another combined into one person. If your spouse does not bring you into a place to appreciate and cherish you, then you may end up feeling worthless. If your spouse does not know how to value your worth, talk with him/her and inform them with what you have need of.

More importantly, seek God for favor with your spouse. Keep God's Word precious in the depth of your heart to guide you to all favorable things. Walk in the truth and have mercy toward your spouse. When you do not understand their actions – pray about it so you both can talk it over. If you find yourself quarreling, stop and pray, because you may speak something that you can later regret.

It is remarkable that the warning in Proverbs 18:21 precedes the blessing in Proverbs 18:22.

Proverbs 18:21 (KJV) 21) *"Death and life are in the power of the tongue: and they that love it shall eat the fruit thereof."* Proverbs 18:22 (KJV) 22) *"Whoso findeth a wife findeth a good thing, and obtaineth favour of the LORD."*

Know that you have power to speak blessings upon blessings over your spouse. You do not have to hastily speak death or curses, because the husband found his wife, and the wife is a "good thing". Wait, here is the best, the husband finds favor with the LORD. If the husband has found favor with the LORD and you are as one, that favor resonates unto the wife as well. You both can have the favor of God operating within your marriage and that's a powerful thing!

Living life with someone who refuses to change is a recipe for disaster. You can't have one partner constantly growing and changing while the other person remains the same. That's unbalanced and will cause a lot of issues to come about in the relationship. It will make the bond between the both of you unstable.

It's good to be mindful to have the desire to want to grow and get better, not only for yourself but also for your partner. There should be a mutual desire to want to grow and become interconnected, intertwined, and interwoven in order to achieve oneness within the marriage. When two cohabitate, it should be done in total agreement of adapting to an arrangement that benefits those involved. This would include any children that either person had prior to the marriage. That means it will take sacrifice and even dedicating yourself to be understanding.

I believe that marriage is a ministry. That means that it's going to require growth and change from both husband and wife over time. Throughout this union, you will be confronted with an opportunity for change in the areas of each of your weaknesses. It will then be up to you as to how you will respond. Will you accept the challenge to change and get better, or will you be stubborn and refuse growth? We are all on a continual journey of growth in this life. Marriage is a tool to help aid in that growth process. It brings about the growth and maturity we need to become better individuals.

Marriage was intended to cultivate spiritual growth, along with developing strong communication skills; learning how to serve others; and learning how to love on a much deeper level. If you both are growing and prospering in God, that helps your family to grow and prosper in the LORD as well. If you are in agreement with the Holy Spirit, your children will learn to walk in agreement with the Spirit of God also. If you edify one another, you then can jointly edify Christ Jesus, and as you lift up His name, others can be drawn unto Him.

Though you keep personal things private, those who observe your lives, can benefit from your union. If you are a believer, then adhere to the Word of God, for it instructs you in righteousness. 1 Thessalonians

5:5 (KJV) tells us, *"Ye are all the children of light, and the children of the day: we are not of the night, nor of darkness"*. Thus, let your marriage be one of light.

The ministry of marriage is helpful to many. Even if you both are upset with one another, your neighbors should not be able to discern your tempers because as you walk and stand in their presence you should do so in peace. You must be willing to take upon one another's burden to grieve, but to have the other rejoice because of your ability to be supportive to their needs. Ultimately, being willing to change will counteract wanting to remain the same, and you both can excel together. Growth has to take place, and hopefully for the better of the union.

Throughout the ministry of marriage, the LORD is constantly working to help you become better individuals. Many of your bad habits will begin to fall off and you will then develop healthy habits that will not only benefit you but will benefit your partner. So if there is something totally aggravating about your partner, just pray and give it time and without you even thinking about it, the day will come where your partner has been transformed and then you can give all the glory to God for the results! Instead of nagging your partner to change their ways and bad habits, just remember to release your frustrations in prayer to God because only He knows why your partner behaves the way he/she does and only He can work out the kinks.

Men as well as women can be nurturers, but women must allow men to be accountable in their roles. Men tend to strengthen those around them because of their ability to be strong. In most recent decades, women have had to assume the responsibilities of men because of circumstances that somehow forced certain changes within the household, and this has led to women being deemed to be independent and strong.

That is fine but there can be challenges that come along with the title of being independent and strong. As a woman, my mentality became, "I can do everything on my own and I don't need any help from anyone;

especially a man". And this couldn't be further from the truth. I had to learn that I couldn't do it all. I had to come to a place where I had to relinquish my independency upon myself, and learn how to depend on God. God showed me in countless ways of how I could learn to depend on Him. He had to break down that tough exterior, pride, and stubbornness that I had.

I eventually came to a place in my life where I put my total trust in God. Once I put my trust in Him, and believed that he could take care of me and my family better than I ever could, many great benefits followed. If we are not careful, we can start to think that we don't need any help from anyone, and whenever a great guy does comes along, we have to learn how to let a man be a man in the relationship.

We can sometimes tend to think that we are so strong to a point, that we can even drive men away because we won't allow them to be the men that they need to be in our lives. It doesn't paint a picture to say we are weak as women, but there are just some things that we have to allow a man to do and to be able to assume his role in a relationship with us.

Men are the strengtheners and women are the supporters. Look back on Adam and Eve. Adam was intended to tend the ground; Eve was his help mate. If a couple know their rightful place in the marriage, growth can be wonderful. If you have tendencies to be domineering – relax and let the man handle those heavy loads – just do it in agreement.

Be willing to support one another's opinions and do not disregard what the other one perceives of a situation. Let him say to you "Honey, here is how I think we should approach this matter". Try to listen to what he is saying. Don't disrespect his role and become argumentative, just take the time to listen and if you do not agree, just simply try to respond in love; do not retort.

This will allow for the next conversation to be discussed with more consideration and respect for how the other person believes, perceives, and receives information. When you trust in the LORD with problems encountered within your marriage, you will not give your power to outsiders. When you decide to take your problems to your family and friends, you can began to start a whole other war. You don't need people on the outside of your marriage discussing your problems at their dinner table, or talking about you behind your back. Please don't turn to social media for support to have others take your side when you're in a brawl with your spouse. This will not turn out for the good of your marriage.

If you take your marital issues to the LORD, they will be secured within God's ever-loving hands, and there would be less fighting over issues and less input from the outside of the marriage. When the course is not set for failure, then the path of destruction is not trodden upon. So it's best to remember, to prevent is to avoid. You can avoid a whole mess of failure when you realize you have the power to prevent the destruction.

You have now established a course of history with your spouse, therefore, frequently review the beginning of that history. Recall to one another what sparked your interest with each other and identify the concepts and precepts that catapulted you to the altar. When you stood at the altar to say your vows, you made a three-strand cord covenant that included you, your spouse, and God. It is the two of you who will exemplify characteristics that are linked to the attributes of God. The more you both allow God to use you for His purpose and His glory, the more you both will personify His qualities of love.

Yes, God has the ultimate ruling in your marriage, but the two of you must seek Him simultaneously. You live together, so now talk together; walk together; and arrive as one in your accomplishments. If you both agree on counseling to help you along the way, that is fine. There's nothing wrong with having counseling from your Pastor, but there should be a limit on whoever else should be informed about your marital issues.

You have to protect your sacred union at all cost. Your marriage is sacred, and so is your beautiful union. It should not be taken for granted or tossed around for anyone to take a stab at it. Once we have something so precious and near and dear to our hearts, we should protect it at all costs. When most people decide to enter into a marriage, they may not be thinking about the many potential problems that may lie ahead, and that is why marriage should be entered into with sober thinking, and counseling. The evaluation of yourself is most important because being sober in mind will have you examine yourself to permit an honest view of who you are.

Will you be honest with your findings? You may have some deeply, rooted issues, then again maybe you do not. However, the important thing is to first be honest with yourself and then ask the FATHER what He sees in you in case you are missing something. Find a reflection of yourself in His Word, for He knows all about you. Psalms 139: 1-4 (KJV) tells us, 1) *"O LORD, thou hast searched me, and known me. 2) Thou knowest my downsitting and mine uprising, thou understandest my thought afar off. 3) Thou compassest my path and my lying down, and art acquainted with all my ways. 4) For there is not a word in my tongue, but, lo, O LORD, thou knowest it altogether."*

Perhaps, you will realize how great it is and well worth it, to be patient and wait on the right person. Then you will be able to find comfort in the vows that you are preparing to make before the LORD and your mate. We can have a tendency to think that marriage will provide perfect happiness. A strong misconception of marriage is that the person you married will solve all of your problems; such as, you won't have any more financial struggles; and you will be able to have sexual gratification all the time, but marriage is so much more than that.

God designed marriage for spiritual connection; partnership; a means for maturity; to pursue God as a union; to raise a family, and in regards to sexual expression, it is to build intimacy. A marriage reflects God's covenant relationship with His people. Marriage is not about finding someone who will take away all of our problems or complete us in every way. When we view our partner as such, we have now crossed the line over into idolatry because only our Creator can complete us in every way and make us whole.

"Make me complete," oh what an earnest desire. Actually, no one can complete you because you are a complex, intricate, and uniquely designed person by the Almighty God. It is He and only He that can make you complete, however, the concept is not too far to reach, it's just a bit misleading. You should have someone that compliments your existence. That person need not to modify you or make you over; they will just need to accept you for who you are and you both will grow together as one. When we look to people to complete us, they will disappoint us every time. Why? Because we are imperfect beings and that type of demand should never be put on another human being because they have just as many flaws as the next person.

Once again, it is sad to know that in today's society, marriage is no longer being honored. Some people tend to give up on their sacred union far too easily, but the antidote is far more precious than the poison, because when the resolve is to remain together and work through the complicated situations of marriage, it supports the declaration of your promises to stay together for better or for worse.

If you stay married long enough, you can conquer and defeat "the worse" and rejoice in the better times, so take heart because you are not in the marriage alone. God is your Advocate. He will fight for you, but He wants us to fight for one another too, because *"What therefore God hath joined together, let not man put asunder"* Mark 10:9 (KJV).

God does not divorce us on our worst days. Yet, is He caring, comforting, and compassionate to see us through to help us to grow within Him. He does not throw in the towel when we are unloving, yet He patiently waits for us. He loves us through our messiest days and seasons. Sometimes it will be that our hearts may be hardened towards our spouse, but remember, you once had the hope within the core of your heart to be married to your husband/wife; so why not let hope guide you to remaining with that person.

The worst days may come, but better days will lie ahead. *"Weeping may endure for a night, but joy cometh in the morning"* Psalm 30:5 (KJV). If you have hope for your marriage, then you must believe that your marriage will get better, despite the statistics and the naysayers. Remember, marriage is a gift from God. *"Every good gift and every perfect gift is from above, and cometh down from the Father of lights, with whom is no variableness, neither shadow of turning"* James 1:17 (KJV). Did you receive your spouse as a gift from God? Your perception makes the entire difference of how you can celebrate your marriage. God is love and marriage is just another way for His glory to be shown in all the earth!

BECOMING ONE

Have you ever noticed how couples who have been married for many years often seem to resemble each other? They can even tend to finish each other's sentences. They can almost know exactly what the other one is thinking and how their spouse will react to any given situation. They have so much history together and they even tend to feel like the other is an extension of themselves.

It has been proven scientifically that couples can have duplicated features after spending years together, however, the biblical perspective expands beyond facial features, behavior patterns, and so forth. In respect to the Bible, when two become as one, the ideal is that they can function as one person. Once you and your spouse have gotten married, the two of you are now on a journey of becoming one in everything! Do we really know what the process of becoming one requires of us? Getting married is not simply taking vows and promising to love each other forever, but it's truly becoming one body; one flesh; and one in agreement.

Beyond the marriage vows is the basis of your covenant. You both have agreed to walk in agreement as one before our Holy FATHER. The harmony that shall exist between you both will strengthen and encourage you throughout your marriage. Philippians 2:1-4 (KJV) states, " 1) *If there be therefore any consolation in Christ, if any comfort of love, if any fellowship of the Spirit, if any bowels and mercies,*

2) Fulfil ye my joy, that ye be likeminded, having the same love, being of one accord of one mind. 3) Let nothing be done through strife or vainglory; but in lowliness of mind let each esteem other better than themselves. 4) Look not every man on his own things, but every man also on the things of others."

The above scripture pretty much explains what becoming one is all about. Though the scripture speaks inclusively to all who will believe; it can also be used for individuals learning on how to walk as one, therefore, to become as one from a spiritual standpoint, you both must have a relationship with Christ Jesus.

Many people may not be believers of Christ, but, whatever your faith may be, it is best not to be unequally yoked. You should have the commonality of being focused and guided by the same values, morals, and principles. Talk and discuss what your faith beliefs are prior to getting married. If you are both on the same path, then you both shall have spiritual harmony and this will allow you to walk together without condescending challenges that one is failing to believe in the correct aspect. You should both fellowship together in the Spirit. You both should be committed with compassion. Seek to find ways to exemplify the compassion of God. Rather than complain about the shortcomings of your spouse, you can encourage one another with empathy and be kind and merciful with humility.

Do not dwell on your past relationships or experiences with others but focus on your new union together. That is also not cleaving to your mother and father's rules and governances, but talk and discuss how your home is to be governed and establish the rules you find to be important. Set goals and celebrate your accomplishments with each other.

Both of you should embrace the joy about your future together as one, so try to remain excited and allow the light of Christ to illuminate your relationship. You can review and practice Christ commandments together; also, allow Christ to abide in you both and keep His Word ever abiding in you. The both of you shall also think in the same capacity of being likeminded, so allow your minds to be like the mind of Christ.

If you find that you have more differences than similarities, then ponder on the things that you do have in common. Philippians 4:8 (KJV) gives good advice on things to focus on; *"Finally, brethren, whatsoever things are true, whatsoever things are honest, whatsoever things are just, whatsoever things are pure, whatsoever things are lovely, whatsoever things are of good report; if there be any virtue, and if there be any praise, think on these things"*.

You two should have the same love with the same sacrifices for one another. Something that most people do not think about are the words they can use to either edify the other person or destroy them. You must remember people love based on how they know how to love. The more you sacrifice for one another, the more your love is appreciated by each other.

During the most recent decades, it was commonly stated that "you cannot change a person" and for the most part you really cannot. The object is not that you change them, but that they change the things that need to be, because of being married to you. Instead of constantly asking God to change your spouse, consider this; He may be using your spouse to change you.

You both are not to be conformed to the world but renewed by the transformation of your minds in Christ Jesus. Avoid things that make you resemble the world and just be yourself. Don't be filled with bitter and spiteful emotions toward one another, but be more concerned about your spouse than yourself. The remarkable thing is that you both are more than conquerors in Christ Jesus, so pray together to stay together.

After vows have been spoken and performed at a wedding ceremony, husbands and wives come together in sexual intimacy, where they will now seal the deal. They are becoming "one flesh". *"Therefore shall a man leave his father and mother, and shall cleave unto his wife: they shall be one flesh"* Genesis 2:24 (KJV). The consummation of the marriage does involve the intimate connection that you will have with one another. Not only is this intimacy shared between you and your spouse, but it is also shared with God. Yes, God is even involved in the love-making act itself! He created it and He desires that the husband and wife both enjoy each other along with themselves in this beautiful act of love. Here is where God allows us to express our love for one another in a most intimate way.

When you invite the LORD to be a part of this amazing act, it can be like having a whole other experience with your partner. There is no problem in the bedroom that God cannot fix, so if you get to a place where you feel like things are fizzling out in the bedroom, pray and ask the Holy Spirit to aid you in rejuvenating one of the most special and intimate acts that He has created.

Throughout this intimacy, the LORD is weaving the two of you together. It is like the three-strand cord that is not easily broken. If you ever wonder why divorce is often so painful, it's because of the tearing apart of a cord that was so tightly woven together. If the two of you are now one flesh; one body, as the Word of God says, imagine having your body being ripped apart. That would be very painful because now it's like the one body being pulled apart into two separate bodies once again.

You wouldn't want to bring excruciating pain to your body, so you must view your marriage and your partner as your own body. It is best said this way, *"In this same way, husbands ought to love their wives as their own bodies. He who loves his wife, loves himself. After all, no one ever hated their own body, but they feed and care for their body, just as Christ does the church"* Ephesians 5:28-29 (NIV).

If Christ is faithful in feeding, nurturing and taking care of the needs of the church, we also must be faithful in taking care of our spouse in the same sense. The way that you care for yourself, care also for your spouse. If you are hungry, you will feed yourself. If you are wounded, you will bandage yourself. If you're feeling down, you will encourage yourself. What you do for yourself, do also for your spouse. Love them; cherish them, and treat them well because they are a gift from God.

As the two of you live your life as one, you will share everything with each other. You share your successes; failures; hopes and dreams; as well as your possessions, money, and so on. There is no one without the other, and through this oneness, couples should be building each other up and supporting one another throughout their union. They are taking into consideration the other's needs and caring for them in every way that they possibly can.

This oneness also demands God's direction and design for each of your lives. God has great use for the married couple in His kingdom. They can accomplish great and mighty works through Christ Jesus. The two can easily fulfill their God-given duties when they work together as one. They can also experience success in their common goals for family life, work and ministry. It is good that you both have a mutually, supportive attitude to build a powerful union and a home filled with the love of God. Always keep in mind that marriage was patterned after Christ's love for His church.

We must understand that there is a common goal when two began as one. Our overall accomplishment involved with marriage is to become one flesh. Many people have trouble with comprehending this concept but even by science and physical law it makes sense that the two can become as one. When life is conceived, the donation of the male's life source connects with the receptive egg of the female for fertilization. If life is reproduced, the two involved generates a baby. This is proof in the natural world that two become as one but in the spiritual sense, the two become one when they walk as one. When we trust in God, we therefore believe in God. When we walk in accordance with His will, His will shall abide as love in our hearts. Husbands, with the love of God in your heart, shall you love your wife. You must learn to walk with her, and she with you – as the two shall be as one.

While speaking on the topic of becoming one, let's turn our focus on Adam and how he came to reference God in his becoming one with Eve. God gave Adam the unique, precious gift; the first of its kind. Adam called her – WOMAN! Adam delighted in the LORD – He obeyed God until the day he laid down his life spiritually for Eve and disobeyed the command of God. In the beginning, Adam had within him the spirit of obedience. He had not defied God, and nor was he opposed to God. As a matter of fact, God had placed within Adam the gift to reverence Him.

You must be able to see the spiritual character of Adam before he decided to be accountable for the love of his life. Adam was empowered with love, joy, peace, and patience. Since Adam was to lead all and be an example of how to glorify God, the Creator, does it not make sense to know that Adam had no sin in himself? However, he arrived at a place where he became the very opposite of our Savior.

We know that the devil, in his cunning ways persuaded Eve to disobey God, but the fall of man did not occur because Eve ate of the tree. Yes, she would die surely as God told them the result would be, but the command was not given to Eve, it was given to Adam. Let's ponder the love that Adam has for Eve. He has said, the two shall become as one flesh, so how does Adam make such a profound declaration only to negate it with bifurcating himself from Eve? When Satan approached Eve, we are not given a time frame on how many times he tried to persuade her. It would be a worthless argument because of her actions, but think about it, how many times are we tempted by the enemy with the lust of our eyes, flesh, and pride of life?

God made Adam so that Adam would be the example of how mankind was to acknowledge, exalt, and worship God in the beauty of His Holiness. Adam was not made with sin lurking within the parameters of his mind, nor did he refute any commands given him by God. Therefore, we do not know how long through the day that Adam and Eve spent together but we do know that Eve was persuaded by the enemy to disobey her husband.

The charge was never laid to Eve, it was only conveyed to her by Adam, so ponder this, Eve loved Adam and God; Adam loved God and Eve, and God loved them both. Adam was accountable for Eve. Though male and female were created in the image and likeness of God, they had a free will. They had the gift to reverence and obey God, but in their ability to make free-will decisions, this led to disobedience.

God made provision for Adam and Eve because He was their FATHER. When we have children, we want our children to obey our rules. Rules are made to discipline and govern us. They help us to remain within the borders of safe love; if we abide according to the rules. When our children disobey, they only have us to come to and make their report, unless someone else is harmed by their actions or deeds, but nonetheless, they eventually must come to us and confess what they have done.

Once the approach happens in the garden and the persuasion occurs, Satan poses the question to Eve sarcastically; Genesis 3:1 (KJV) *"Now the serpent was more subtle than any beast of the field which the LORD God had made. And he said unto the woman, 'Yea, hath God said, Ye shall not eat of every tree of the garden"*? Satan knew that tree was off limits to Adam and Eve and they had not eaten of the Tree of Life, but Satan did not tempt Eve to eat from the Tree of Life, because at that point there was no sin of disobedience within her and had she ate from the Tree of Life she would have been immortal without sin.

Adam was not given instruction to not eat from the Tree of Life, but only from the Tree of Knowledge of Good and Evil was Adam forbidden to eat of. Since Satan knew Adam had the spiritual authority, he did not challenge, or choose to confront Adam in this case but he targeted Eve, as she was in a state of innocence. With a childlike mind of innocence do we often find ourselves trusting the wrong persuasion? Again, we do not know how long Satan was after Eve, we only knew she eventually gave him a response. Genesis 3:2,3 (KJV) 2)*"And the woman said unto the serpent, "We may eat of the fruit of the trees of the garden: 3)But of the fruit of the tree which is in the midst of the garden, God hath said, Ye shall not eat of it, neither shall ye touch it, lest ye die"*.

Eve had the knowledge, but she did not have the wisdom. Eve responded by confirming information that was given unto her. She, like a child said, "we shall not eat it, or touch it or we will die". Satan hates man, and he was destined to destroy their relationship with God. He was bitter because of his own arrogance, defiance, and ignorance. He knew being kicked out of Heaven was one of the worse punishments to encounter and to be jealous of God's love for man, he retaliated. He then replies to Eve with a lie because he knew to die meant separation from God, so now Eve is manipulated and takes a bite from the forbidden tree.

Let's explain that tree for a moment. God has infinite wisdom, intelligence, knowledge, and power; He knows every possibility, and probability. He knows that He is All Loving, All Life, All Truth, and All Power. He knows every mathematical causation and scientific effect and therefore, God is ABSOLUTE. Since God is Absolute, He also knows there is an opposite of everything He is. That of course is exemplified in Satan.

Satan is all hatred, all death, all lies and weaknesses. Satan is the epitome of division whereas God is total unity. The Tree of the Knowledge of Good and Evil, stored within it, is the information of all that God is and all of who Satan is. That tree contained information that was too much for our minds to comprehend.

Eve, was tested and tried. How many of us can say we surpassed every test that has come our way? We cannot, because we have the nature of Adam within us. Adam did not fail because he bit the fruit, Adam failed because he loved Eve and by his own words he said the two would be as one. Since Adam had to honor that which he professed, he had to be accountable for his other half. When Eve gave Adam the fruit, he did in fact eat of it, but here is something to consider. Since Adam knew he and Eve was as one, could half of him be condemned? No. Should Adam and Eve be in combat against each other? No. Since Eve had eaten of the tree, if Adam had not, then Eve would sustain death alone.

Adam's vow was that the two should be as one. How could he watch her then perish and go on to live in the Garden without her? She was his helpmate. She belonged with no one else but Adam. If Eve had to suffer for her disobedience alone and die – being separated – would God have given Adam another helper? We do not know because when we come to realize this is a foreshadowing of the Love of Christ – we must take into consideration the love story. John 3:16 (KJV) *"For God so loved the world, that He gave His only begotten Son, that whosoever believeth in Him should not perish, but have everlasting life"*.

Romans 5:7-12 (KJV) *"For scarcely for a righteous man will one die: yet peradventure dare to die. But God commendeth His love toward us, in that, while we were yet sinners, Christ died for us. Much more then, being now justified by His blood, we shall be saved from wrath through Him. For if, when we were enemies, we were reconciled to God by the death of His Son, much more, being reconciled, we shall be saved by His life. And not only so, but we also joy in God through our Lord Jesus Christ, by whom we have now received the atonement. Wherefore, as by one man sin entered into the world, and death by sin; and so death passed upon all men, for that all have sinned"*.

Now in respect to Adam and Eve, we are told in 1 Peter 4:8, *"And above all things have fervent charity among yourselves: for charity shall cover the multitude of sins"*. Since charity is love, we come to note that love covers a multitude of sin. Yet, Adam could not forsake Eve and tell her that she was on her own. He loved her so much; he gave his life for her by disobeying God.

Adam knew no sin until he tried to cover Eve's sin because he loved her. That is the difference between Adam and Christ; that he was not perfect; whereas, Christ had no sin ability within Himself. He knew His purpose and therefore, He had to fulfill a prophecy that would save the world. Adam's sin brought about condemnation for all mankind.

Christ took upon our sins: 2 Corinthians 5:21 (KJV) says *"For He hath made Him to be sin for us, who knew no sin; that we might be made the righteousness of God in Him"*. Christ is God and therefore, He had the power to defeat sin and its counterpart death. He prayed for us because He loves us. He prayed that we, as His Bride will be one with Him and God.

John 17:20-26 (KJV) He prayed for all believers: *20) "Neither pray I for these alone ,but for them also which shall believe on Me through their word; 21) That they all may be one; as Thou, Father, art in Me, and I in thee, that they also may be one in us: that the world may believe that Thou hast sent Me. 22) And the glory which Thou gavest Me I have given them; that they may be one, even as We are one: 23) I in them, and Thou in Me, that they may be made perfect in one; and that the world may know that Thou hast sent Me, and hast loved them, as Thou hast loved Me. 24) Father, I will that they also, whom Thou hast given Me, be with Me where I am; that they may behold My glory, which Thou hast given Me: for thou lovedst Me before the foundation of the world. 25) O righteous Father, the world hath not known Thee: but I have known Thee, and these have known that Thou hast sent Me. 26) And I have declared unto them Thy name, and will declare it: that the love wherewith Thou hast loved Me may be in them, and I in them"*.

Therefore, we see how love conquers and procures mercy. We come to understand that man is not perfect but that perfect love is within Christ Jesus. Jesus prayed that we be one with the FATHER in the spiritual sense, but you must pray that you and your spouse be one in the earthly realm. Pray that you both be dedicated unto the love of God in your hearts, and that you keep Christ as the center of your relationship. Pray that you find the contentment of His peace when test and trials are upon you, and you both take His hand and seek truth together. Love; think; and walk as one.

UNDERSTANDING THE BROKENNESS WE FACE

There will be imperfections and inhibitions that will be discovered regarding your spouse throughout the duration of your marriage. As the old saying goes, "you don't really know a person until you have lived with them". Though you may have discovered some things about your spouse during the courtship phase of the relationship, there are still things that may unfold during a marriage that could be concerning.

If your spouse has ever experienced any situations or circumstances that has had a lasting negative effect; you may begin to see the results of those effects that has resulted from a traumatic past event. If there were any past traumas, hopefully your partner found healing and restoration from it, but if not, hopefully they will be up front and honest on how such traumatic events have affected their lives.

We can try to hide our brokenness from our partners for only so long but eventually the pain from our past hurts will begin to surface throughout the marriage. It's a good idea to have an understanding of the brokenness that we all, as humans face, but please know that no matter what has happened in your past, you are not broken beyond restoration.

When two people come together in one household, it is so important to understand that you are now taking on the other person's mentality;

personalities; habits; and even possibly generational curses. You both are integrating your behaviors and patterns to become woven into the future of each of your lives. Your baggage of weaknesses can even possibly become the weaknesses of your spouse.

Generational curses are sinful habits that are passed down from one generation to another due to rebellion against God. If your family line is prone to the habits of alcoholism; anger; divorce; drug abuse; incest; or any other ungodly behaviors, and you witness any of these traits within your spouse, there is likely to be a generational curse involved.

The Word of God describes theses deeds as generational consequences being passed down from one generation to another. *"Keeping mercy for thousands, forgiving iniquity and transgression and sin, and that will by no means clear the guilty; visiting the iniquity of the fathers upon the children, and upon the children's children, unto the third and fourth generation"* Exodus 34:7 (KJV).

The sinful habits that we inherit can easily have a negative effect on us and on those whom we are in a relationship with. Since we learn by behaviors, we must realize that our families' negative influences can cause inner conflict within us. This includes how deeply we partake in sinful practices, and yet, we must come to a place within ourselves and decide that we can choose to either travel the road of curses or the road of blessings.

The Bible says that our consequences are tied to the choices that we make, therefore, we can either choose life and blessing, or death and cursing. *"I call heaven and earth to record this day against you, that I have set before you life and death, blessing and cursing; therefore choose life, that both you and thy seed may live"* Deuteronomy 30:19 (KJV).

We never have to settle with going down the same road as our parents, nor our ancestors. For instance, the child of an alcoholic father who has suffered neglect has an option to change the course of his life.

Though it was a consequence of his own father's behavior; this pattern can end, but it must begin with that individual.

What about the brokenness that we may have faced in our childhoods? We may have grew up with issues resulting from our youth; things that we never told anyone about. If such traumatic events have happened to us and we never received any counseling from those things, we can carry them throughout our adulthood, which oftentimes lead to more issues in our lives.

With a study of how our brokenness can affect our relationships, I've decided take a look at a few examples of what some people have gone though and even dealt with in their marriages:

While growing up, there were people who had witnessed one of their parents being oppressed and abused by the other parent, and they found out that, that mindset had transferred into their way of thinking without them recognizing it. Some people were abused as a child and then grew up with tendencies to abuse others. Some people found that while being single, they drank excessively and used this as a coping mechanism for their stress and pain, but once they were married, they desired to continue in their bad habits. They found that those bad habits caused them to go into a drunken rage, which resulted in them abusing their spouse.

Some people found themselves experiencing abandonment and rejection issues over the years as well. Some of those individuals never accepted that they had any problems and went through life assuming they were fine, but it doesn't mean that those issues will just go away on their own. These things are detrimental to the overall being of an individual. If people never receive the proper healing and deliverance needed to make them whole, those issues will resurface and begin to cause a lot of damage to the individual themselves and to the ones that they have committed to spend their lives with. Once the issues resurface, their spouse will then begin to witness the brokenness that stemmed from their traumatic past.

It is important to try to address as many issues as possible within our lives and seek the help we need before involving others to come be a part of our lives. Surprisingly, past impacts can linger when a person suppress their fears and may be uncertain of how to express to their partner of how neglect and abandonment is an ordeal for them. If your spouse was sexually abused as a child, it is possible that they may be bombarded with tormenting facts about their life that involved the robbing of their innocence.

Some people have had other unhealthy habits such as gambling. An addiction to gambling can result in neglecting priorities; being irresponsible as a partner; as well as not giving attention to the needs of the family. Most gamblers are away from home, days at a time. Sometimes, people will use gambling as a way to escape their problems and the responsibilities of life.

While growing up, some people may not have been taught how to manage and save money. As an adult, they found themselves lacking the ability to practice self-control with their finances. While being single, they didn't give much thought to properly managing money since they didn't have a family to care for, but all of a sudden, they found themselves married with money management issues and often found it difficult to embrace their responsibility to manage finances for their family. Money issues have been a major reason behind many divorces.

Being married should motivate people in breaking practices that are unhealthy mentally and physically. If you are now married and have a family, and you have been honest with your spouse and confessed any strongholds, that is one thing; but if you have habits that you have not been honest about, you owe it to your spouse to discuss these matters. Bad habits can disrupt your family lives and cost you peace in your own home.

Another cause of withdrawal could stem from an inadequacy because of rejection. In my young adult years, I dealt with the spirit of rejection. It can rob you of your joy and peace, and make you feel worthless and unloved. These issues will soon be discovered and if not dealt with accordingly, they will then become burdensome to the spouse. We cannot rescue people from a place where only God can deliver them from. We cannot bandage wounds that only God can heal. We cannot suffer for pains that only Christ died for. We cannot be a spouse superhero because God set the standards needed for our loved one's healings, so allow God to use you for His glory and exemplify the love He knows your spouse needs. Hold tight to the reins, because God can use you to help your spouse to know that they are not alone, but that they are loved.

We must seek to understand the brokenness that our partners face. It's good practice to try not to judge them. We shouldn't belittle or ridicule them, because there is hope for everyone. We must realize that we can't fix our partner's inner issues, but it's good to know the One who can and His name is Jesus. He knows exactly how to fix the brokenness that we face because He knows exactly what broke us in the first place.

If you are aware that your inner brokenness is causing issues within your marriage, please know that there is help available. When you want to be a better person for your spouse and children, it will be evident because you can then begin to grow. There are some people who refuse help for whatever reason or another, and they deliberately desire to make others miserable because they are unhappy, but remember, misery loves company and hurt people, tend to hurt others.

In our state of brokenness, we tend to hurt the ones closest to us. Most of us may not mean to do so, but these unresolved issues in our lives have a way of coming to the surface and causing us to act out in a way that is oftentimes hurtful to the ones we love. Our brokenness can cause us to say and do a lot of hurtful things to our loved ones, and this is the reason that it will take much forgiveness and patience to love someone through their broken state and the process of becoming restored.

When we examine our own flaws and issues, then we must become considerate that our spouses have much to deal with about their flaws and issues as well. This will be a daily occurrence of matters that can either be resolved or last a very long time. People can become weary if they are not willing to be supportive about the matters that caused the brokenness initially. Galatians 6:9 (KJV) *"And let us not be weary in well doing: for in due season we shall reap, if we faint not"*.

Though you may sometimes encounter challenges with your spouse on a week to week, month to month, or year to year basis – be not discouraged. Being committed to love someone throughout their brokenness takes a lot of work. The work that you're committing to will take a lot of prayer. Prayer is powerful; prayer changes the outcomes of current situations. The committed work will also take much forgiveness, patience, and understanding.

Another issue couples face because of their brokenness, is avoiding honesty. They may have become so use to hiding truths that they do not identify with their faults; this is called denial. This is an even bigger problem when one of you are too stubborn to admit or recognize your faults; especially if one lacks a desire to be healed.

You can seek the LORD on revealing your area of weaknesses and be willing to allow Him to deliver you of such things, because you should desire to have a healthy and thriving marriage, but how can you have that when you may be the very one standing in the way of achieving that positive outcome?

As women, we can sometimes nag unnecessarily about what our partners are doing wrong or not doing at all. At one point, in my own relationship, God began to show me that there is no need to nag a man about his issues. 1 Corinthians 14:40 (KJV) instructs believers to *"Let all things be done decently and in order."* For example, I desired that my partner love me the way I wanted him to love me, and do things the way that I wanted them to be done, so it was easy for me to go to him and point out all the things he wasn't doing to show his love for me but the LORD help me see that in doing so, it would only tear him down as a man; it would break his spirit and only cause strife in our relationship.

In relationships, we don't often think of the weight that our words carry and how they affect the other person. The Word of God says that *"Death and life are in the power of the tongue"* Proverbs 18:21 (KJV). We have the ability to either tear someone down or build them up with our words. It may not always be easy to be the bigger person but you can choose to build up your partner instead of tearing them down. *"Above all, love each other deeply, because love covers over a multitude of sins"* 1 Peter 4:8 (NIV). Love always win.

We have no idea of how to fix someone who is broken inside, so why not trust the Manufacturer, (God), who made the individual? Only God knows why we all act the way we do and why we tend to treat people the way we do, so why not put your trust in the LORD in dealing with your partner? God knows how we all have been mistreated in our past by those who have hurt us deeply, and He knows the depth of the damage that was done to us. It will take the love of the FATHER to do the patient work of healing and deliverance to help get us to a place of wholeness. Only the FATHER can make the crooked places in our lives straight. Psalms 147:3 (KJV) states, *"He healeth the broken in heart, and bindeth up their wounds."*

When we entrusted God to send us a spouse, we did so soberly. We had a hope to be woven into a bond of love that would last until the end of our lives with our mates. Christ said in Luke 12:48 (KJV) *"But he that knew not, and did commit things worthy of stripes, shall be beaten with few stripes. For unto whomsoever much is given, of him shall be much required: and to whom men have committed much, of him they will ask the more."*

In the event people have experienced the woes of life such as abuse; neglect; poverty; and rejection; these occurrences in your life cannot be reversed because of the actuality that they actually happened! You cannot fix someone whose been abused. Only God can heal the wounds and fix the brokenness inside of an individual.

You cannot hope money will resolve an impoverished mindset; it is only your faith, hope and trust in an all-loving Holy FATHER that provides for your needs. Nor can you stomp out rejection, but you can be restored to acceptance into the heart of your spouse by the power of unconditional love by God being at the heart of your marriage. It takes the work of our Creator who designed us and knows why we are broken; to be able to complete the work of restoration, healing and deliverance within our lives, and only He can bring us to a place of wholeness.

Thus, having trusted in our FATHER, shall we then doubt Him to know what is therefore best for us? Philippians 4:19 (KJV) states *"But my God shall supply all your need according to His riches in glory by Christ Jesus."* We must therefore believe and walk in that trust because Christ has made us to be more than conquerors in Him!

Working on your relationship with your spouse, can take a lot patience and a lot of work that you must be committed to in order to have healthy; thriving marriages. Relationships can be really difficult at times, and we know that neither of us are perfect, therefore I believe that it takes much prayer to witness change come about in each of our lives. Romans 8:37 (KJV) *"Nay, in all these things we are more than conquerors through Him that loved us."*

If you keep God as the center of your relationship, you have a much better chance of your marriage surviving. Marriage is not easy, and as stated before, commitment requires forgiveness, patience, prayer and work. It is a great practice to go to God in prayer when we want to see change come about in the lives of the ones we love.

Once that change happens within your relationship, you can then glorify God for what only He can do. The Word of the LORD says, *"But when you pray, go into your room, close the door and pray to your Father, who is unseen. Then your Father, who sees what is done in secret, will reward you"* Matthew 6:6 (NIV).

If you examine your relationship or marriage, and feel that you are repeating a generational curse, be encouraged because those curses can be broken and it can start with you! You can be the one who stops the generational curse by choosing life. Your family may have a history of a certain sinful trait, but you are not bound by this generational curse.

You have a choice to either continue in the footsteps of your ancestors which will pass along the curses to your children, or you can become the curse breaker in your family linage, so that you can bring an end to the curse and not have it affect your children, nor your children's children. God has a plan for your freedom that will shatter the chains of those generational cycles! He has redeemed us from the curses being passed on from one generation to the next. This redemption comes as we understand that the root of our problems is in the spiritual realm.

When the time comes for us to apply God's Word and power to our lives, we can make the conscious decision to walk in righteousness and obedience to God, and therefore, the chains of bondage will be broken. The freedom we have longed for can be ours! Choose to be a curse breaker so that you can experience the true freedom that Christ died to give you. Recall, Romans 8:1 (KJV) *"There is therefore now no condemnation to them which are in Christ Jesus, who walk not after the flesh, but after the Spirit."*

SPIRITUAL WICKEDNESS IN HIGH PLACES

The Word of God says, *"For we wrestle not against flesh and blood but against principalities, against powers, against the rulers of the darkness of this world, against spiritual wickedness in high places"* Ephesians 6:12 (KJV). "To wrestle means to take part in a fight, either as a sport or in earnest, that involves grappling with one's opponent and trying to overthrow or force them to the ground" (Oxford Languages Dictionary). Now here is the epitome of spiritual warfare. When the scripture says that we wrestle not against flesh and blood, it is telling us that our fight is not with one another. It's much deeper than you and I can imagine.

In a marriage, when a couple find themselves at odds with one another, they can misconstrue the intent of their spouse. They may also began to think that their spouse is the primary source of their problems, and eventually, they will see one another as the enemy. For instance, if a wife constantly nags or criticize her husband for everything he does wrong and can never credit him for anything he does right, he can then use this as a crutch to remain combative towards her, thus, using her words in memory recall and allowing himself to remain in a defensive position. The husband may often point the finger at his wife and say she is the source of his stress and all of his problems. If the husband falls into this snare from the enemy, he can then place the blame on his spouse, thus, never resolving deeper issues.

Another example would be where a husband may purposely do things to sabotage his wife's success because he's jealous of her accomplishments and less time that he may have with her. Today, men are not as challenged as much as they were in years past. There was a time when men were the primary source of provision for the home. Many men met their obligations to be the one who worked long hours and made sure that the essentials for the home were provided for. Nowadays, more women are the owners of their business and are achieving much success. When jealousy is prevalent, people will distrust their spouses and become resentful. In the above scenario, the wife may begin to feel discontent with her husband, and this will invite more disagreements, discord, and disharmony.

The wife, in due time may begin to perceive her husband as an enemy instead of the real enemy at work here. When a married couple is not in fellowship with God and one another, they can easily fall prey to the evilness of Satan's devices. She doesn't see how the adversary is persuading her husband to rob her of her joy, and she, therefore, is disheartened about his reactions to her success. This nemesis is not her husband; the real opponent is a spiritual enemy.

What we must understand is that it's not the person themselves that we are at war with, but it's the spirit within the man or woman that is at work and is bringing confusion and strife to the relationship. *"For God is not the author of confusion, but of peace, as in all churches of the saints"* 1 Corinthians 14:33 (KJV). Confusion and strife is of the enemy and if you have a lot of this in your relationship that means that the enemy is in the midst. The enemy operates through the individual, causing the repeated behavior, or offense to the other party.

The Word of Ephesians 6:12 reminds us here that once again, we do not war or wrestle against flesh and blood which is humanity in itself, but against principalities (rulers); against powers (authorities); against the rulers of the darkness of this world (world-rulers); against spiritual wickedness (wicked spiritual beings) – which are fallen angels, demons, and Satan himself; in high places. This world is Satan's domain. He is described as the prince of the power of the air. There are many evil spirits, but in this regards to such a spirit of deception that are working cunningly; then we must realize that it is not our partner that is acting out against us but that there is something else at work.

The highest place in your physique is the crown of your head. Your head houses your mind in the brain, therefore, it is in the mind where the enemy is planning to overthrow the throne of your marriage. It is important to read the Word of God to get understanding of this wicked, spiritual activity that exists in high places because our battle is not physical; it is spiritual. Once we grasp this understanding, we can now know how to engage in warfare the correct way.

In this fallen world, we are at war with a real enemy who hates us and he hates marriages. If there's a crack in your relationship, it's a way for the enemy to enter in and wreak havoc between you and your spouse; causing you to be at war with one another. The enemy will often use people who are especially close to us to launch an attack against us.

Evil in high places emphasizes a battle beyond this world. Evil never sleeps; it never rests. Proverbs 4:16 (KJV) speaks of evildoers *"For they sleep not, except they have done mischief; and their sleep is taken away, unless they cause some to fall."* Evil spirits are always looking for ways to sabotage and destroy relationships. 1 Peter 5:8 (KJV) warns, *"Be sober, be vigilant; because your adversary the devil, as a roaring lion, walketh about, seeking whom he may devour."*

Since we now know that we are at war with a spiritual enemy, we must also know what the Word says about protecting ourselves and how to engage in war the correct way. The incorrect way to engage in war would be to argue; fuss and fight; yell, and even abuse our partners but Ephesians 6:13-18 (KJV) says, *"Wherefore take unto you the whole armour of God, that ye may be able to withstand in the evil day, and having done all, to stand. Stand therefore, having your loins girt about with truth, and having on the breastplate of righteousness; And your feet shod with the preparation of the gospel of peace; Above all, taking the shield of faith, wherewith ye shall be able to quench all the firery darts of the wicked. And take the helmet of salvation, and the sword of the Spirit, which is the word of God: Praying always with all prayer and supplication in the Spirit, and watching thereunto with all perseverance and supplication for all saints."*

You can now see how God is giving us instructions to be able to stand and wage war against our enemy. You should never feel helpless against the battles you face but to know that you have the Word of the living God to help you fight your battles; while praying and helping your loved ones in the midst. When there is a waging battle going on, sometimes you will just have to stand still and see the salvation of the LORD God Almighty fight for you (Exodus 14:13). God can do more for you by you just trusting in Him, rather than getting yourself involved in something that may not even be your battle. Understand that some battles are not yours, but the LORD's (2 Chronicles 20:15).

Our fight is not just within our relationships and marriages, but the enemy will show up and try to attack us through other people in our family; our friendships; associates at work; and so on. The enemy is after our Christian witness and our ministry. He loves to try to bring us out of character. Our character is very important because it represents our LORD.

For instance, the enemy knows that if he uses someone to agitate me to the point where I am extremely irritated, I will become very angry. Anger has been one of the generational curses that was passed down through my family linage. If I become angry, the enemy knows that I have a tendency to lose self-control and begin to allow words to come out of my mouth that I can't take back. The LORD helped me see that once my words have gone into the atmosphere, then there is no taking it back. The Word of God says *be ye angry, and sin not: let not the sun go down upon your wrath:"* Ephesians 4:26 (KJV).

When we become angry with our spouse, we can say some very hurtful things. We can say things that we can't take back. Before separating from my ex-husband, we got into such a heated argument and we both said things to each other that hurt each of us deeply and we knew that once we said those things, then the internal damage was done. There was no taking back our words. Jesus is precise about this deed; He states in Matthew 15:18 (KJV) *"But those things which proceed out of the mouth come forth from the heart; and they defile the man."* We must practice living in accordance with the Word of God and utilize wisdom because no one else owns our power to be self-controlled.

Our enemy studies us and he knows what pushes our buttons. Once my temper is elevated, I know that the enemy wants me to lose my cool; say hurtful things; and destroy my witness. He wants me to allow my anger to destroy my relationships, but I am now reminded that in 2 Corinthians 10:3-4 (KJV) states *"For though we walk in the flesh, we do not war after the flesh; For the weapons of our warfare are not carnal, but mighty through God to the pulling down of strongholds."* Indeed, my anger was a stronghold, but praise be to God that our weapons of warfare are mighty through God to destroy our strongholds!

It's no difference when we are on our jobs: the very ones who observe believers are also the ones who try to antagonize us. They tend to get on our last nerves until we get upset and lose our cool. There are people who wait to see if we will lose our temper so that they can say "I thought he/she was a child of God".

The people who oppose the Spirit of God, also hate the children of God, but the Spirit within us prevails against the spirit that is within them. Someone is always ready and waiting to point a finger and accuse us, therefore, we must be careful not to destroy our witness by being tempted by the evil one.

Now going back to our relationships, you have to realize that your partner is not your enemy and to combat the real and invisible enemy, you must use your weapons of warfare and that is to pull the Word of God out of your arsenal. By using our weapons of warfare, this will be the way that we win the battle and take down our formidable foe. God has given us everything we need in this life to be victorious over whatever our enemy tries to bring our way; even in our relationships.

You are not just protecting yourself from the snare of the enemy, but you have a responsibility to protect your spouse as well. You must stay prayed up for their sake as well. If you look at your spouse and you see him/her suffering with pain, or going through a horrific ordeal, stop and pray because that is an attack of the enemy.

When you hear despair in their voice, encourage them to look to God from which cometh their help. There may be a time when you both will encounter test and trials to place you at odds with each other, therefore, use the authority in the invested blood of Jesus Christ and command those spirits back to hell. Ephesians 6:12 empowers us with wisdom to know who we are in Christ Jesus. So many people are being defeated by the devil within their relationships, but you have the power to tell Satan that he cannot have your spouse, nor your marriage.

You must remember the two is as one. That being the fact, when 1 is divided by 2, the result is a half. You are not halved, you are one with each other. You devour the enemy when you stand as 1; pray as 1; live as 1; and are not divided by the chaos of the evil one. This is a war, but thanks be to God that Christ has already defeated and overthrown the kingdom of darkness.

Daily, we tend to deal with periodic; demonic onslaughts, but as we stay prayed up, we may be able to stand our ground when these attacks come our way. Remember, it's not always the person on your job who doesn't like you, or some kind of acquaintance who's jealous of you, but often times it's the one closet to you that the enemy will try to use to attack you.

The Word in Ephesians 6:14, also tells us that our loins should be girt about with truth. Prepare yourself with the truth of God's Word. This proves that you are fortified, steadfast, and unmovable. You are united in a holy matrimony and your vows are sacred! Even through the brokenness, your hope should remain in Jesus Christ! Know this, God ordained and positioned you both for victory as one; unified for His glory. Don't just sit idly by, allowing the fiery darts of the enemy to take you and your spouse down, but always stay armed and be ready because the enemy never stops. He may go away for a moment but he will eventually try you again.

As you put on the breastplate of righteousness, understand that this represents a holy character and moral conduct before the LORD. We should always want to represent our LORD in the best way possible and at all times. So even if someone tempts you, let your light shine ever so brightly, because this will send a message to your enemy that you are not backing down but that you are armed with righteousness and that you are fit for the fight.

In Biblical times, the Roman soldiers wore special shoes called caligae on their feet which allowed them to move quickly during battle. Caligae is a heavy-soled, hobnail military sandal boot. Not only did these shoes greatly protect their feet but it allowed them to advance against their enemy. These shoes helped to make the soldiers prepared and ready to run into battle. *"And your feet shod with the preparation of the the gospel of peace"* Ephesians 6:15 (KJV).

I no longer use my feet to run into battle being improperly armed and ready to hurt others, nor do I retaliate and use my mouth to tear them down. I have learned to fight my battles on my knees through prayer, before the LORD. The LORD lovingly helped me understand that it's better to be prepared with the preparation of the gospel of peace.

Anger and strife never solves any issues for us. God knows how to handle our enemies far better than we can. We don't have to retaliate against anyone who hurts us. Don't destroy your witness, just continue to show the love of Christ to those who hurt you and allow God to fight your battles. He is our Advocate!

If you notice that your spouse continually does things to agitate you or to bring about a struggle in the relationship – begin to pray for a deliverance to come upon him/her. Analyze their motives, and if you discover a reasoning for their intentions, then you have more reason to pray. Is he/she under the influence of the accuser, making suggestive thoughts unto them? Then pray that God covers their ear gate and protects them from subtle instructions. Remember, you don't have to engage in the warfare with your spouse, but you can make the conscious decision to handle it in a way that will bring change and an opportunity to give God the glory.

By arguing with your spouse; avoiding them, or mistreating them, you are inciting your husband or wife to vexation. This is contrary to the love of God and that's only adding fuel to the fire. You are then yielding to the enemy and that's what our enemy wants. His purpose is to cause a division amongst the two of you. If the enemy can *divide* the both of you, he will ultimately *conquer* a complete separation amongst you two.

Rather, if you trust God and motivate your heart to abide in Him, and stimulate your mind to think on Him, eventually you will find yourself surrendering all unto Him. James 4:7 (KJV) says it this way, *"Submit yourselves therefore to God. Resist the devil, and he will flee from you."* Try to remember that when you engage in heated fights and arguments with your spouse, the enemy wins. At this point, you are not helping your spouse, you're only hurting him/her. So instead of retaliating against your spouse, combat the problem through prayer. Through prayer is how you win the battle; retaliating is how you lose.

When you understand the need to have prayer incorporated in a marriage, then you can understand how to combat the enemy against his schemes and attacks. Prayer is a powerful tool and is much needed in many marriages today. Many times, prayer is the last thing that people will often turn to when dealing with marital issues, but prayer is the tool that you can use to help them at any given moment. We must understand that the enemy hates marriages. He hates love. He hates anything that's good. He especially hates Godly relationships and will stop at nothing to try to destroy them.

Here is a significant point, since you two have become as one, you can then pray as one; fast as one; and walk as one. When you recognize that the evil one may be using your spouse to cause strife between you two, gently suggest a fasting time and be sure to ask and allow the Spirit to direct you both. Jesus said in Mark 9:29 (KJV) *"This kind can come forth by nothing, but by prayer and fasting"*. Pray aloud with one another on one accord. If you have yearned and hoped that your marriage would survive the attacks of the enemy, then pray and fast.

If you ever wondered could your marriage make it through the storms of life, and your desire is that both of you will get better, trust God so that you can have a stronger marriage and even began to speak it in the atmosphere. If you are experiencing turmoil at the present moment, that's no reason to throw in the towel or give up on your marriage. If your relationship doesn't look like what you want it to be right now, then speak positive affirmations to your marriage and speak what it will become.

If you seek God about your marriage and He assures you that it's going to get better, take Him at His Word. Have faith in God that your marriage will get better. Taking on the shield of faith as stated in the above scripture will help you take God at his Word and believe his promises concerning your marriage.

Being at odds with your spouse is exactly what the enemy wants. If you really love your spouse, fight for them through the power of prayer and the Word of God. Marriages are worth fighting for. Remember that marriage is a beautiful depiction of who God is and that He intends for you to love and enjoy one another to the fullest of your union.

If you don't understand the fight at hand, the enemy can easily sneak in and destroy the very thing that you prayed for. It's a fight to protect what's yours but the good thing is that you have the LORD on your side helping you to fight and win your battles. Putting on the armor of God is so vital to helping you survive and thrive in your relationships and marriages.

GIVE YOURSELF PERMISSION TO BE SINGLE

Ladies and Gentlemen, if you are currently living in a season where you are single, assure yourself that it is ok. Some people cringe at the thought of being single but the Word of God in Isaiah 41:10 (KJV) explains that God does not want us to fear if we are alone: *"Fear thou not; for I am with thee: be not dismayed; for I am thy God: I will strengthen thee; yea, I will help thee; yea, I will uphold thee with the right hand of my righteousness."* Therefore, by giving yourself permission to be single, means that you are willing to be content with just you and being content with who you are during this season of your life.

When you find yourself in a season of being single, it is a great time to focus on yourself in a healthy way. It's ok to take time to rediscover yourself. Rediscover your dreams and goals; hone in on what you're good at and even passionate about. Ask yourself, "What is it that I really want to achieve in life"?

There is power in rediscovering who you are and what you were created to do in the earth. God made you for a specific purpose, therefore you were destined to contribute something into the earth. We are all just passing through this life and it's important with what we do with the time we are given, therefore, we can't afford to waste the time we have on earth because life can be very short.

When we get older, we can sometimes look back on our lives and say "What did we do with our life" or "What did we do with the time that we were given"? I would often hear people say that if you go by the graveyard, there are many people who took their talents, gifts, and dreams to the grave. For some reason or another, they never found an opportunity to become all that the LORD had planned for their lives.

Being single gives you a chance to really focus on what you were created to do. There is so much that we all can contribute to this world if only we would focus and even believe that we were created to do amazing things in this life. To encourage yourself, let the Word of God in Philippians 4:13 (NKJV), *"I can do all things through Christ which strengthens me"* resonate in your mind and spirit.

There is no greater time spent than time with God during this season of your life. You can get to know Him on a deeper level without so much distraction in your life. Ecclesiastes 3:1 (KJV) states *"To every thing there is a season, and a time to every purpose under the heaven"*. Many people do not know what season they are in. They think it to be only by mere chance that they have arrived at a place of being single.

Oftentimes, when we are involved in relationships, we can tend to solely focus on the other person, while taking care of them and making sure they are content. There's nothing wrong with that but we should be careful to not neglect ourselves in the process. Oftentimes, we can even lose our own identity in the person we are dating. It's good to do a reality check to make sure that we are not losing ourselves while being involved with others.

During this season of your life, take all of the stresses of being single off the table. Instead of being anxious about entering into another relationship, take this time to decompress. This is a time to speak healthy unto yourself and to have spiritual conversations with

God. Simply breathe and say, "I am going to be just fine". If you are not with anyone, it does not mean that you should feel stressed out or even become depressed. Simply encourage yourself and confirm daily that this is not the end of the world.

This is just a season of your life that you are now journeying through, so take this time to love and learn more about yourself. It's a time to become whole so that when the right person comes along, you will be fully ready. During my single years, I drew closer to the LORD and began to work on my relationship with Him. There was a whole new revelation that opened up about my life.

God can do so much with us when we are single. James 4:8 (KJV) states *"Draw nigh to God, and He will draw nigh to you"*. It is God who will ordain your season of marriage but He must prepare you first. Therefore, use this time to become efficient with everything He is revealing to you about your purpose.

Do not dwell on the fact that you are not involved with someone. It seems that some people feel they must have a partner to fit in or else people will judge them. There is so much pressure in today's society to be partnered up. Romans 12:2 (KJV) instructs us in this manner, *"And be not conformed to this world: but be ye transformed by the renewing of your mind, that ye may prove what is that good, and acceptable, and perfect, will of God."*

The more we are conditioned to think in agreement with the world, the more we are destroying ourselves internally and spiritually. To focus on what the world thinks of us has led so many people into bad situations. People have succumbed to the pressures of getting involved with someone because it is expected of them to be in a relationship.

I have known many women with the mentality of "I will take any kind of man, as long as I have a man." This kind of attitude has led many women down the path of getting involved in relationships that have had negative impacts, such as abuse, and domestic violence situations. Some women were even afflicted with STD's, all because they chose to relinquish their bodies to a man who had no consideration or respect for them, nor their bodies. Then there are some women who attract freeloaders; they live off of the women's livelihood and do not contribute anything to the relationship. Unfortunately, having a low self-esteem often encourage these futile decisions.

When it comes to wanting to get married, ladies, don't be so anxious to get married that you allow red flags to blind your view. You must totally check out the guy whom you are ready to make lifelong vows with. The Word of God says, *"Do not be anxious about anything, but in every situation, by prayer and petition, with thanksgiving, present your requests to God"* Philippians 4:6 (NIV).

God stipulated how we are to be involved with one another in regards to men and women and their behaviors. That being said, we should adhere to His examples of covenants by marriage. Why do we allow people to serve us up short from what God has intended for us? Why do we often find ourselves giving our partners benefits that only married couples should have? There should be limitations for what we offer the people whom we are only dating.

Since marriage eradicates fornication between men and women, then avoiding fornication can therefore reduce the probable chance of transmitting diseases, thus, preventing diseases eliminates the consequences of disobedience. We were not meant to ravage our bodies; run rough shod over one another's hearts; nor ruin the minds of others. In my opinion, if a man or woman doesn't fear the LORD, that says a lot about his/her character and who they are. Are they perfect because he/she does fear the LORD, no, but at the end of the day, if they do, it should speak volumes about how far they will go to show obedience unto the LORD.

It's so important to take our time and make sure that we really know the person that we are getting ready to spend the rest of our lives with.

We can sometimes be in such a hurry to say "I do", but do we really know what we're saying and do we really know with whom we are saying our vows to? It's alright to be picky when you're considering getting married. Thoroughly check out the man or woman to see if they really want to be married. In the case of a man not wanting to get married, it could simply be that he may not want to be rushed into it.

If this be the case, respect the man's decision. Don't try to force him into marrying you or don't cause him to feel like he will lose you if he doesn't propose to you. There's a reason why some men may not want to be in a hurry to be married and you owe it to yourself to know why. If he doesn't want to be married, it's best not to force the issue because this could cause him to later resent you and that could lead to abuse as well as divorce if he does go ahead with marrying you.

There was a time when I was in my early 20's and I was so in love with this guy that I wanted to marry him. He would say that he wanted to be married too but for some reason he was dragging his feet on the issue. We never got married but later on, things were being revealed to me about him that I thank God that we never got married. Turns out that he had issues with his mother while growing up. He would disrespect her and even began to be abusive towards her. Eventually he turned abusive towards me as well.

While dating, take notice of the red flags that you see and don't ignore them. If the guy that you're dating doesn't want to be married, guess what, another man does, and would be glad to make you his wife. Noticing the red flags, but continuing to stay in the relationship with that man, is where some women tend to go wrong.

Some women will just settle being a man's girlfriend for years and even give him everything that a wife gives to her husband, only you don't have a commitment from him. This is the time to realize your self-worth and to know that you are worth being someone's wife instead of settling for less. If he doesn't treat you as a child of God that you are, you have to keep it moving. Don't be afraid to be single until the right one comes along.

Ladies and Gentlemen, you both need to investigate and probe your partner. Be sure to discuss topics that will affect your overall stability, such as, do you both want to have children? If either of you have children prior to your involvement, are both of you willing to receive the other's children as though they are your own?

Some people do not want to have children. Whatever their reasoning is, the choice is theirs. Both of you should be honest and open about this topic. This is important to know because you don't want to end up in a marriage where you or your children could be at risk of homicide or abuse because your spouse never wanted to have children to begin with.

I know this may be hard to hear but these are real issues where all too often we hear about situations in the news where the person has killed their spouse and children. It's important to be patient and take your time to get to know who you are involved with. There should never be a race to the altar, but instead, take as much time as you need to get to know the one whom you are considering marrying. You want to be sure upon dwelling together, that the home will be a haven. Encourage yourself to wait on the right mate. While waiting, work on loving and caring for yourself.

Give yourself permission to be single without feeling bad about it. Don't allow your family, friends, or anyone else for that matter to make you feel bad or awkward about not being in a relationship. Some families pressure their loved ones to be in a relationship because they don't want to see them alone. You may even have those type of friends who try to set you up on blind dates every chance they get. You need to first be content with who YOU are. Make sure that you are capable of loving yourself before trying to love someone else.

Take the time to enhance your qualities; examine your abilities, and explore your femininity or masculinity. You want to prepare to be appropriately positioned in your marriage, so invite the Holy Spirit in to help you develop your skills of communication; being loyal; being honest; or whatever area you feel that you may be weak in.

In a season of being single, it is currently all about you and God, therefore, get as much wisdom as you can. Proverbs 19:8 (KJV) advises us to obtain wisdom and understanding which applies to us all. *"He that getteth wisdom loveth his own soul: he that keepeth understanding shall find good"*. It's spiritually healthy to become wise in who you are.

Self-care and self-love is important. How can someone love you if you don't love yourself? How can anyone value your worth if you do not exemplify any integrity, principles, or scruples? Spending time with the LORD presents a great opportunity to understand that the Great Physician is at work and is ready to aid you in the areas of your brokenness, if you so allow Him to work on you.

Being single is usually just a season. Your season may be a couple of months, a year, or even longer, but regardless, if the season lasts awhile, you can learn to enjoy the precious time that you have been given and just know that God is working behind the scenes on your behalf and is doing more than you realize.

Eventually you will meet someone if that's your heart's desire and also if it's the will of God, so don't panic. Don't become depressed or even feel like it's the end of the world. If you begin to feel desperate and even act out of desperation, you can begin to make bad choices. This can cause you to stray onto the wrong path and lead you into a relationship that may be damaging to your spirit and soul.

As you take the time to get to know yourself better, be encouraged that this is a good thing. You would think that most of us know ourselves pretty well. After all, we have been attached to ourselves throughout our lives, but you will be surprised to know that most people don't even know themselves as well as they think they do.

I learned how significant quality time is when it is spent with God. He began to reveal the plans that He had for me since before the beginning of time. It blew my mind because I hadn't realized the depth of how much He loved me and how much He desired to make me better on every level. I began to understand who I was in Him and what I was created for. It gave me a purpose and a new outlook on life.

During my single years, I found out so much about myself. I discovered that I wanted to become an entrepreneur! Many ideas and some witty ideas started coming to mind. I even discovered that I had writing skills. The LORD began to put it on my heart that one day I would write a book! I remember one day I started writing and found out that I actually enjoyed it! So I began writing and today I am an author! What a difference it makes in finding out your purpose! What great plans does God have for you? As you spend time with Him, you will be amazed to find out what plans He has for you!

God also helped me to see that out of my pain, came purpose. I was abused in some of my past relationships and today, I am the CEO of a women's shelter where I can help provide information and resources for others who have found themselves in abusive relationships. God will turn your pain into purpose if you allow Him to.

What we go through is not just about us, but it is to help others along the way who have found themselves faced with some of the same battles that we have faced. Please don't sit on the things that God has required of your hands in the earth. Allow Him to get the glory from your story. The pain from your past will set someone else free. Be encouraged to go forth to accomplish those things that God has called you to do. Somewhere, someone is waiting to hear your story on how you overcame the obstacles in your life. Somewhere, someone is waiting on your invention. Somewhere, someone is waiting for you to take your place in the earth and bring forth that which God has purposed in you!

I recall as most people do that when being young, we do not see the grand scheme of things. We would imagine how we wanted things to unfold during our lives. We have our plans; and then there's God's plans for our lives. God's plans are without gaps and voids. *"For I know the plans I have for you, declares the Lord, plans to prosper you and not to harm you, plans to give you hope and a future"* Jeremiah 29:11 (NIV).

I began to wonder how I had spent so much time chasing after things and people that were not a part of God's plan for me. When I began to understand His plan, things in life began to make more sense. I began to have a real sense of purpose in life; and with that, it began to awaken some things within me that I never knew were there.

During my single years, I also found that I had more quiet time where I could hear from the LORD who helped me discover the gifts that laid dormant within me. It was truly a revelation! The more time you spend with the Creator, the more is revealed to you. After all, He created you and He knows very well how He designed you to be and He knows the gifts and talents that lie within you, waiting to be known by all.

While dating, there can sometimes be a lot of noise in our lives that can overshadow the things that God wants to whisper to our spirit. He wants to reveal deep things and even sacred things to us. If we never take the time to spend with Him, we can miss out on so much that He wants to give us. We can become so consumed with proving ourselves to the one we are dating and neglect the most important Person of our lives. If God is our first love, then He should never be neglected, and our hearts should be inclined to His voice.

When you're single, you have more time to focus on things that need to get done. For example, you may have had a business idea that you put off for years. Now would be a great time to do research and began putting together a plan to start your own business; your own daycare; organization; car dealership; hair shop, restaurant, and so much more. The sky's the limit for you once you discover who you really are and what you have the power to do through Christ Jesus!

Another advantage to being single is you can determine your likes and dislikes. Try challenging yourself to do something different. Try doing some things that you may have once thought of doing but didn't have the time and now that you have the time, you can do it. Believe that you are well deserving of some self-rewards, and compensate yourself for the times you neglected your desires while you were involved with someone.

We don't have to wait until someone come along in our lives to start having fun; have fun now! Take family trips and even take a trip with your single friends; take yourself out to eat; go shopping when you can afford to; go explore things that you've never done before or have never thought of doing; surprise yourself and make the best of your single life!

Give yourself permission to be happy and embrace the joy within! Life is too short for regrets and being bitter over what was and what used to be. Find your inner peace. There is so much living and exciting things you can do, so go get busy doing those things! There is a life out here waiting for you to come live it, so be good to yourself.

Also, do not think or believe a lie that there's something wrong with you because you're single. It just may not be your season to meet the right one yet but don't allow anyone to make you feel bad just because you're single. After all, I would rather be single and happy than to be in a toxic relationship and miserable.

As stated before, you won't be single forever unless you find you absolutely enjoy it and desire to stay single. If that be the case, there is nothing wrong with that either but just know that being single forever may not be in the cards for you. God creates us to be relational and to be a part of great relationships.

God said, *"It is not good for the man to be alone. I will make a helper who is just right for him"* Genesis 2:18 (NLT). This scripture does not pertain to men only. *"He created them male and female and blessed them. And he named them "Mankind" when they were created"* Genesis 5:2 (NIV). Trust God and seek His best for your life.

As you seek God, He will provide His best choice that He has for you. However, you must be willing to wait for who the LORD will ordain to be your mate. As you are seeking Him for guidance, ask God to reveal specific details about that person. This will help you discern when that specific person comes along. We don't always know what's best for us but our heavenly FATHER does. As you are patiently waiting for whom the LORD has created for you, do not settle for anyone less worthy of you.

Ladies, God wants to give you His best! You are His DAUGHTERS! Please understand that you are valued in the sight of God! Therefore ladies, do not be so anxious for a man that you end up with Mr. Bozo instead of Mr. Boaz. To get the full understanding of what a type of Boaz is, I encourage you to read the book of Ruth, in the Bible where it gives great details and insight to a type of Boaz.

Gentlemen, God wants to give you His best as well. You are His SONS and He loves you very much! You don't deserve to be with just any woman; you deserve a virtuous woman; a God-fearing woman! Don't be so anxious to just go out and find any woman, but be sure and know that when you have found the woman that God has ordained for you to be your wife, know that you have found a good thing!

Sometimes we don't know what to look for in the one whom we would like to date. What we may believe to be good for us, may not be the best, however, we must be careful to trust God to provide the best mate for us. Ladies, please become obedient to the will of God.

If you read about Sarah in the Bible of Genesis 21, she was an elderly woman and God opened her womb upon becoming obedient to God. Don't you know that He can do the same and so much more for you?

The one who was designed for you is closer to finding you as each day passes by. Ladies, you do not have to search for him, so stay away from dating websites because there are many predators, waiting to take advantage of women who are looking for love. It is very easy to link up with a total counterfeit so remember, it's not for you to go find him, it's for him to find you because the Word of God says, *"He who finds a wife, finds a good thing and obtains favor from the Lord"* Proverbs 18:22 (ESV).

It is important on so many levels that we seek the LORD for our life-long mates. *"Do not be equally yoked with unbelievers. For what partnership has righteousness with lawlessness? Or what fellowship has light with darkness"*? 2 Corinthians 6:14 (NIV). Meeting the wrong person and marrying them can be like stepping into a nightmare that you can't seem to wake up from. If you are a Christian, naturally you should want your partner to be a Christian. You both should be equally yoked so that you give no place to the devil to come in and wreak havoc on your marriage.

When you consider what a yoke is, a yoke can be described as a crosspiece that is placed over the necks of two animals; such as two oxens for instance. The animals will have to pull the load that is attached to them. The two animals are to work together to balance out the workload. In the case of an "unequally yoked" pair of animals, one animal may be weak and one may be strong. Or one could be tall and the other may be short, but either way, they are unequally paired. Because they are unequally paired, the load that they are trying to pull causes them to go around in circles. They are unable to complete the assigned task before them. Instead of them working together, they are constantly at odds with one another.

There have been many people who discovered that they were married to the wrong person at some point during their union. Daily, they experienced agony, anguish, and anxiety because their marriages were not in the will of God. Some of them even stopped living unto God and began existing only to try to find an escape from the reality of their hell.

If you are a believer and your spouse is not, the enemy will have a field day with you. The enemy within the non- Christian spouse will always find ways to create strife and tension within the marriage; causing you both to go around in circles of your issues and never seeming to come to a place of resolution, and this type of marriage have often ended in divorce.

Here is a serious caution against relationships and fellowshipping with those whom you are unequally yoked. Those who are in communion with God, must have no communication with the unfruitful works of darkness. We must develop a proper understanding of the evil of sin, and the precious role of our Savior, which will help us to perceive the justice of God in all things.

In order to have a successful marriage I strongly believe that you should reverence God and allow the Holy Spirit to be highly active in your marriage. He is the one who will help aid the both of you throughout your journey with one another. He knows the brokenness that each partner has within and only He can deliver and heal that brokenness that will ultimately benefit the other.

Isaiah 40:31 (KJV) is a great reminder to wait for the LORD in all things. *"But they that wait upon the LORD shall renew their strength; they shall mount up with wings as eagles; they shall run, and not be weary; and they shall walk, and not faint."* If people guess about your situation, so let it be, for as long as they are spectating, that you remember to *"abstain from the very appearance of sin"*. 1 Thessalonians 5:21 (KJV) tells us to do this regardless of what others think about us as believers. When people label you or accuse you of something because you have been single for a while, *"Fret not thyself because of evildoers..."* Psalm 37:1 (KJV).

Let them know that you are perfectly fine with being single until the right person for you comes along. You must not worry about accusers and know this, every accusation is false and comes from the devil. Remember, the LORD will fight your battles so there's no need to argue with anyone about who you are or what you're doing. Don't waste your breath feeling like you owe someone an explanation.

Do not be afraid if you feel that you have gotten a little older; haven't met the right one; gotten married, or have even had children yet. No need to fret, but be encouraged. The peace of God will guard your hearts and mind, and keep you from worrying and thinking that time will pass you by without meeting someone and being able to start a family. The LORD is mindful of the time and we don't need to put any limitations on Him. He is not slack in His promises concerning you, so even if you have gotten a little older, that doesn't stop God from blessing you.

Age doesn't matter with God, He still desires to bless you so don't give up on your dreams. People of all ages tend to meet their mate and become married. No matter how old you think you are today, you are still not too old to meet the one who was designed specifically for you. If much time has passed, consult with the LORD to make sure that getting married is in the plan for you.

No matter what the fear of being single is all about, never allow fear to drive you into the arms of someone who was not specifically designed for you! Again, be willing to wait for God's best and NEVER settle for less! These are two very important things to consider when you're single and waiting for that special one. Always remember, you are a child of the Most High God. When you consider who you are and that you are of His Kingdom, you'll begin to set your desires higher.

If you have had sexual intimacy with multiple partners, ask the LORD to sever all soul ties and connections with any previous partners. Repent, and look to God and petition Him in this manner according to Psalm 51:10, 11 (KJV) *"Create in me a clean heart, O God; and renew a right spirit within me. Cast me not away from thy presence; and take not thy holy spirit from me."* That way you will not have the anxiety of bringing baggage from your earlier situations into a new relationship with a spouse.

There are people who are currently in bad relationships because they were either too impatient or many have settled. Many of them don't even know what kind of individual they deserve. If this be the case, then there is still an opportunity for a person to seek God. They should ask of the LORD to first help them become who He wants them to be. Perseverance is a spiritual diligence that allows faith to grow you into becoming a better person. Being desperate does not help because it is an emotional hindrance. Bad decisions only lead to prolonged heart aches and pain, so please do not be hasty to become involved with someone.

Let me talk with the ladies for a moment here. Again, it's very important to know your self-worth. Do not allow your desires for a man to cloud your judgement. I remember a time when I wanted to be with this particular guy so bad that I made the wrong decision in being involved with him and it cost me a lot of unnecessary pain and time lost on a relationship that was never meant to be. You have to decide if someone is worth your time and is worthy of you. You have the right to distinguish who is better to lead you in a Godly way, and not only should you discern the kind of man whose worthy of you, but discern the kind of man that will father your children.

I believe we can all testify to some bad relationships that we have encountered along life's path. Some women found themselves involved with men who settled in their homes and would not work or contribute to anything in the home but yet didn't mind taking advantage of all of her benefits. I have known of a relationship where the man exemplified no accountability to God or the woman with whom he was in a relationship with. His mind became idled and Satan incited him to attack one of the woman's children.

Eventually, the child went to the mother and told of the molestation but the woman was not compassionate to the robbing of that child's innocence, and chose to remain in the relationship for fear of losing her man. Too often there are women who are confronted with horrible situations in which they deny the truth, or they end up hating themselves because of the evil they invited into their homes.

Such dysfunctional relationships should have no place in your lives or your homes. If you are a single parent, please think enough of your children to not bring any sexual predators into your home. I believe most people have made some type of bad decision concerning people that they have dated throughout their lives, but at some point you must learn from previous mistakes and how not to repeat those errors. If you know how to make better choices, then you will do better, but you must be willing to put a stop to the dysfunction in your life.

Ladies, know your worth! Learn to love you first. Don't allow Mr. Wrong to come into your life and take advantage of your mind; your body; your dignity; your money; and whatever else you may consider offering up to him. Your sacrifice is not to any man that you are not married to. Your obedience is unto God, and you should not be willing to sacrifice your relationship with the LORD for any man. Please read and study the counseling of God in His Word; for surely the instructions are evident and His standards guide the way. Psalm 119:105 (KJV) states *"Thy word is a lamp unto my feet, and a light unto my path."*

Men can tell when women are gullible and don't have any self-worth about themselves. There are men who prey on such women. They know that if they mistreat you, you are willing to continue to let them be a part of your life. They will laugh and talk about you behind your back and even tell their friends how they mistreat you and how you still want to be with them.

Do the math. If that man you love is doing more subtracting than adding to your life, he is not the one. It is time to re-evaluate the relationship. Count your loss and move on. Ladies, know your worth! You are precious to God. He loves His daughters very much and He always wants what's best for us.

There are people who have never received proper healing or deliverance needed to keep a healthy relationship. You would be amazed at how many people are in relationships that shouldn't be because they are broken on the inside. They don't love themselves and therefore, they mistreat those whom they get involved with. They have lived shattered lives and do not care about destroying the lives of others.

Some people won't even remain single long enough for God to heal and deliver them; instead, they walk around leaking. They leak past traumas and hurt; running from one relationship to another when they should be running to a relationship with God. These people don't need just any kind of relationship, they need a covenant relationship with God so that they can get the help and healing that they desperately need.

People who seek counseling that is God based and driven, can bring positive outcomes, but when the spirit of a person is desecrated and violated, the wounds are deeper and more dominant. Searching for a person to bring you out of your misery will not work. They may tolerate you; but in all reality there is only One who can truly heal and deliver us from our brokenness and that's Jesus!

Having time to heal from a place of destruction means you must rebuild your values, morals and worth. If you have been through such a horrific ordeal in your life; your body may be stressed, and your mind may be confused about your perpetrator. You may ask yourself, "How did you allow such behavior to cause such pain"?

Revive and live from a place of healing and do not hop from one relationship to another. If you are leaking past hurts, rejections, and traumas, disallow yourself to look for bandages to hide the pain and suffering. We cannot conceal our wounds from Jesus. He knows all about it, therefore, seek the LORD for total restoration.

From time to time, Jesus would retreat alone to a place where He could pray and spend time with the FATHER. If you have found yourself in a season of being single, the LORD may be trying to draw you away from the riff raff to spend some intimate time with you so that He can heal the wounds from such dysfunctional relationships that you may have allowed yourself to be involved with. He desires to love on us; teach us; deliver us, heal us, and make us whole.

We all tend to go through seasons of loneliness but it is worth it to just wait rather than rushing into something that you may later regret. When we petition God to send us the kind of person that we want, let us understand nobody's perfect. We may not get everything that we want in a person but God always know what we need. We know that there is no perfect man or woman. As you talk with the LORD about the kind of mate you want, just keep in mind realistic goals.

Ladies, see yourselves as the Daughters of the Holy and Righteous King. When you have a healthy self-esteem about yourself, you won't just hook up with anybody just to say you got a man. Oftentimes we miss this point because our self-esteem may be so low that we are willing to accept any kind of man that comes along, or we may not even know what kind of man we deserve. Know your worth and wait for that one who will know and respect the heir to a Holy Throne. He will be able to identify you if only you believe you are a child of God. He will then be willing to love you as Christ loves the Church and gave Himself up for it. (Ephesians 5:25).

Ladies, God wants to bless us with His best but, how can we have His best if we may be internally broken? Many women suffer with low self-esteem and I was one of them. When you have low self-esteem issues, it contradicts the assuredness of you being a child of a Holy God. Your low self-esteem can cause other types of distractions because you are focused upon your outer opposed to your inner self.

You must accept everything that God says about who you are. Build yourself to know He is great in you, and when you begin to comprehend just how much God Himself loves you, oh my! What a fantastic love story you will discover within! So stop defeating yourself all because you may not feel worthy, none of us are – it is all on the Merit of Christ Jesus that we are awarded as being children of God. God is love, and you should declare to love yourself.

Gentlemen, see yourselves as Triumphant Warriors in Christ! You are the hunters and when you're looking for a wife, don't just settle for a pretty face and a nice body but take the time to find out if she has the qualities of being a virtuous wife. The Word of God says, in Proverbs 31:10-31 (KJV) *"Who can find a virtuous woman? for her price is far above rubies. [11] The heart of her husband doth safely trust in her, so that he shall have no need of spoil. [12] She will do him good and not evil all the days of her life. [13] She seeketh wool, and flax, and worketh willingly with her hands. [14] She is like the merchants' ships; she bringeth her food from afar. [15] She riseth also while it is yet night, and giveth meat to her household, and a portion to her maidens. [16] She considereth a field, and buyeth [1] it: with the fruit of her hands she planteth a vineyard. [17] She girdeth her loins with strength, and strengtheneth her arms. [18] She perceiveth that her merchandise is good: her candle goeth not out by night. [19] She layeth her hands to the spindle, and her hands hold the distaff. [20] She stretcheth out her hand to the poor; yea, she reacheth forth her hands to the needy. [21] She is not afraid of the snow for her household: for all her household are clothed with scarlet. [2] [22] She maketh herself coverings of tapestry; her clothing is silk and purple. [23] Her husband is known in the gates, when he sitteth among the elders of the land. [24] She maketh fine linen, and selleth it;*

and delivereth girdles unto the merchant. [25] *Strength and honour are her clothing; and she shall rejoice in time to come.* [26] *She openeth her mouth with wisdom; and in her tongue is the law of kindness.* [27] *She looketh well to the ways of her household, and eateth not the bread of idleness.* [28] *Her children arise up, and call her blessed; her husband also, and he praiseth her.* [29] *Many daughters have done virtuously, but thou excellest them all.* [30] *Favour is deceitful, and beauty is vain: but a woman that feareth the Lord, she shall be praised.* [31] *Give her of the fruit of her hands; and let her own works praise her in the gates.*

Gentlemen, God wants to bless you with His best as well. Men are visuals and can tend to choose women based on their looks; God knows what you desire but your desires for a wife should go much deeper. *"If we hope for what we do not see, we wait for it with patience"* Romans 8:25 (KJV). Wherefore, men, do not settle for a Jezebel spirit but seek to find a just woman. We are children of the Most High King, so let us therefore live in that honor. Our FATHER has all power, and He knows what is best for us.

Gentlemen, consider when you become married, that you are asking to be accountable for others. The point is that you must not only ask God for help, but you must be willing to assume the responsibility of being awarded such treasure. God isn't going to give you His best if you are internally broken and you don't love yourself because if you don't love yourself, how can you love your wife as God loves the church? When you ask God for His best, you may have to go through a little bit of a wait period, and oftentimes it's to prepare you to receive God's very best. Oh, sons of God, what a joy and blessing to know, if you lack anything – God shall provide. When you honor God, He will guide and support you.

Do not shun His hand of mercy over you. He can heal you and strengthen you. The woman that God will bring to you should be treated as a Princess whom is an heir to a Holy Throne. If you have any notions about how you are going to treat her, let it so be as your equal and not your slave. She will be your help mate; she will not be meant as an object. If she is a subject of God's heart, she most definitely should be the melody in yours.

Ladies and Gentlemen, you are God's Sons and Daughters, whom He loves very much! He, therefore, knows the desires of your hearts and can perform any request. Ephesians 3:20 (KJV) says it in this respect, "*Now unto Him that is able to do exceeding abundantly above all that we ask or think, according to the power that worketh in us.*" All you need to do is trust Him.

Acknowledge your season and realize how blessed you are to become prepared for your spouse. Would you not also want the one you will meet to go through a preparation season as well? Can you imagine people who enter into a marriage and didn't take the time to let God prepare them first? Imagine what those people may have to deal with and how patient they will have to be while seeing their partner go through these growing pains.

If we wait on the LORD and be patient enough to let Him work on us first, and strip us of some things before entering into a relationship, we will be better prepared. The LORD desires to work on us from the inside out; building us up in Him, while building our self-esteem and even bringing us to a place where we can have a healthy dose of self-love.

I think at times, we don't often give God enough credit for what He does while working behind the scenes on our behalf. He can do so much with us while we are single if we only give Him the chance to do it. I can testify to the growth that I have received while in my single years. It was just me and God and God knew all about me. He knew the things that made me happy as well as sad. He revealed to me the most inner places of my heart, and He allowed me to commune with Him so that He could better aid me.

He proved Himself because He wanted me to walk in the righteousness that Jesus have so clothed me in. Just as 2 Timothy 3:16 (KJV) states *"All scripture is given by inspiration of God, and is profitable for doctrine, for reproof, for correction, for instruction in righteousness: That the man of God may be perfect, thoroughly furnished unto all good works."* To God be the glory!!!

Honestly, my single years was the best time of my life. I learned so much about my Savior and I even developed a better prayer and study life. I enjoyed every bit of the peace that I had been given during this time. I was able to see the hand of God at work in my life in so many, unbelievable ways. During this time, He also brought a great deliverance and healing to my life. He matured me and taught me so much about who He is and who I was in Him.

I wouldn't trade that intimate time that I had spent with the LORD for anything! When it's just you and Him, it's like having some of the greatest days and moments of your life. I know that I may not have had the opportunity to have this precious time spent with the LORD had I been involved in a relationship because my attention would have been so heavily focused on that individual. My prayer for those who are single, is to enjoy your time with the LORD and allow Him to bless you bountifully while it's just you and Him. Allow His love to take you to higher heights in Him and to even take you to places that your heart could never have imagined.

It is not to say that you can't have these precious times with the LORD while you're married, it's just that sometimes you can be pulled into so many directions with family life and so on. The busyness of life can sometimes keep us distracted from having precious time spent with our LORD but you can still manage to set aside that precious time when you're able. Even when we are in a relationship, it is good practice to remember to set aside some time to get in the presence of a most Holy God. It is well worth it.

I can honestly say that God is my first love. With Him, I feel that there is nothing missing and nothing lacking in my life. He makes me feel complete in every way. At one point in my life, I could truly began to understand what the Apostle Paul spoke of when he said, *"Now to the unmarried and widows I say: It is good for them to stay unmarried, as I do. But if they cannot control themselves, they should marry: for it is better to marry than to burn with passion"* 1 Corinthians 7:8-9 (NIV). At one point, I remember that I had begun to enjoy my single life and time spent with the LORD so much that it almost became a thought to me that if I don't marry again, it is well with my soul.

I think that people owe it to themselves to be honest about what they really want. I've heard people say that marriage isn't for everyone. There is nothing wrong with someone desiring to be single and to stay single for the rest of their lives. I don't think anyone should ever feel pressured to get married for whatever reason; instead, just remain true to yourself of what you really want. If you desire to be married, great! But if you don't there is nothing wrong with the decision you have made. At the end of the day, be at peace with what your heart desires.

If you want a God-fearing man or woman, you yourself must be ready to receive God's best. One thing is for sure, He will not misalign you with a mate. He will send you someone that is equal with you, but still able to help you. I believe that God has great men and women set aside and reserved for those who are ready to receive them.

It must be reiterated that while you are single, get to know yourself and find out your interests. Go pursue your dreams and goals; spend time with your family and friends; love on yourself and treat yourself well. Most importantly, spend time with your Creator. Understand this, that when God begins to speak to your heart, He will also teach you how you are to be treated. *"And the LORD shall make thee the head, and not the tail; and thou shalt be above only, and thou shalt not be beneath;"* Deuteronomy 28:13 (KJV).

Once you discover why you were created and the part you are to play in this gigantic earth, you will be amazed! Spending time with Jesus is well worth it! Count it all joy because you have nothing to lose, but everything to gain in getting to know Jesus more intimately, and remember, if you are in a season of singlehood, it's nothing to be ashamed of, so hold your head up and say it's going to be alright. You have the greatest opportunity for cleansing; healing; deliverance; rediscovering your purpose; and living your best life. You will also be able to discover just how much Jesus loves you which will cause you to love yourself, so that when the time comes, you will be able to love someone else.

"But thou, when thou prayest, enter into thy closet, and when thou hast shut thy door, pray to thy Father which is in secret; and thy Father which seeth in secret shall reward thee openly" Matthew 6:6 (KJV). Embrace the grace; ponder the revelations; become consecrated and motivated to let God lead you in wisdom. This season in which you may have found yourself as a single, should be your season to blossom in the LORD – for greater is He in you. You are okay to be in a season of silence and patience; prayer and fasting – a season of being single. Cherish this time, and if you are already married, allow time for you and your spouse to have that special time with the LORD.

Seasons do change, and by the time you began to discover your purpose and you began living out your purpose while having fun and enjoying life, time tends to fly by and before you know it, the one who was designed for you has now found you. Now you will be ready. You have had time to heal and grow and find your life's purpose. You will be ready to love, because you now love yourself in a much healthier way. And when that right one comes along, they will only be an addition to the amazing person that you are and the happiness that you are already experiencing!

PUT NO ONE ABOVE GOD

When I think about how loving, gracious, and amazing our heavenly FATHER is, it makes no sense to allow someone or something to take first place in our hearts over Him. When it comes to relationships and things that we treasure so much, we can easily do this without thinking about it. Men and women can tend to idolize one another within their relationships without even realizing that they are doing so. Throughout the years I have listened to the conversations of other women expressing themselves about the need of being with a man, and honestly, I can recall a block of time from my past when all I could do is focus on the need to have a man in my life as well.

Some women conveyed their hungers and yearning as desperation and some from mere loneliness. Some women would even assume that they needed a man to make them whole and complete. Over the years, I heard many things ranging from mild conversations about a need for a man, to some outrageous conversations such as, "I need a man and I got to have one now!" Some women can tend to have men on their minds from the time they get up in the morning until the time they go to bed, and vice versus with men. I know this all too well because I used to be one of those women who were heavily fixated on having a man in my life.

I need to be transparent; I confess that I was in the same predicament where my conversations with my friends and I were primarily focused on dating men and constantly thinking from our fleshly desires. It appears men were the primary topic of our discussions. We spent so much time talking about our relationships and the things we did while being with the men in our lives. It was evident that not having a man in our lives was not an option or that our whole world would be revolved around a man if we were involved with one.

Men being the central focus of our discussions, helped us to realize how much control they exercised over us. Depending on how men treated us; that would sometimes determine our mood and they would determine whether we were happy, sad, stressed, or overjoyed. We would put so much emphasis on our men to a degree in which the relationships we were involved in were consuming our lives.

When I believed I was in love with a man, my nose would be wide open, as people tend to say. I found myself submissive unto him, as though I was his wife. Everything that I did was centered on pleasing and satisfying him. It was all about making sure that my man was happy and what he wanted, I would be sure to deliver. I would give him as much of my time as he wanted while neglecting some other important things that I could have been doing at the time. Had this man become an idol in my life?

We as women, have the tendency to love deeply and beyond our own control. It's like our hearts are an ocean of deep love and when we find ourselves head over heels in love with a man, oftentimes you can't tell us much of anything. If there are any red flags, we can barely even see the writing on the wall. In the relationships that my friends and I had, there were times when we had not taken the time to evaluate the terms and conditions of our relationships, nor did we examine if there was a reciprocation of emotions. We just simply gave in to the fantasy of being loved and loving someone.

Overwhelmed with various scenarios, we concentrated on all the strategies to obtain an approval from a man. We even found ourselves giving these men our power. We had sacrificed our power and surrendered our will to men who had no genuine concern for our wellbeing. We would find ourselves living according to their standards, while needing them to validate our value and worth. As women, we can tend to base our happiness on how men can perceive us to be. For this purpose, we may thrive only to realize that we may be just another notch in their belts. I know this all too well because this was a cycle that I repeated when I would look for validation from a man.

Eventually I learned that no man could validate me. Instead of seeking approval from a man, I learned to seek approval from God, and the more I began to communicate with my Creator, the more I began to accept and love myself as He created me to be. *"And He shall bring forth your righteousness as the light, and thy judgment as the noonday"* Psalm 37:6 (KJV).

We can tend to believe that people can give us unconditional love. We seem to think they can confirm our worth and give us the tools to be happy but this is not so, because people are only human. Since we are all flawed and are imperfect beings, there is no way that we can measure up to a level of perfection. Therefore, we must realize that men should not be the center of our heart, but that only God should be the source of our joy.

The agape love is the greatest form of love expressed by God. John 3:16 (KJV) *"For God so loved the world, that He gave His only begotten Son, that whosoever believeth in Him should not perish, but have everlasting life."* The error of loving someone in place of God leads us to make idols of them in our hearts. We should never replace an everlasting love with insubstantial love. Why? Because there is a place within our hearts that was created only for the Creator to reign. Our Creator specifically designed us where there would be a void in our hearts that was only intended for Him to fill. Oftentimes, we will look for people or things to fill this void within our hearts to only end up finding out that they never can.

We love because God created us with the ability to love, but we must understand that man cannot be the master of our love, nor can man be the subject of our desires. Our desires to love must be entrenched through the Spirit of God, meaning when the love for God is embedded within our soul, we will love Him with all our being. Romans 8:5 (KJV) *"For they that are after the flesh do mind the things of the flesh; but they that are after the Spirit the things of the Spirit"*.

Our God is a jealous God and He says, *"Do not worship any other god, for the Lord whose name is Jealous, is a jealous God"* Exodus 34:14 (NIV). If our happiness and contentment is only based on an individual, then it is only a matter of time before that person lets us down and disappoint us in some way or another.

It is perfectly fine to desire being with someone and even fall in love. There is nothing wrong with that because that's how our Creator made us, however, we should be aware when we are loving someone in an unhealthy way. If we as women, put men on such a high pedestal in our hearts, and vice versus for men, we have now created an idol of that person.

Can your spouse become your god? Yes. It is good to love your spouse, but no one should come before God. When we have a realistic view of people and marriage, it will aid us in not entering marriage with the wrong intent. We cannot think that someone will complete us in every way possible. It is impossible. If this is what we believe, then we are sadly mistaken. No one can complete us or make us whole. No one shall rival God in our hearts. *"You shall have no other gods before Me"* Exodus 20:3 (NKJV).

That which we love more than God, or delight in, or even depend on more than our Creator; those people or things have become our god. I have to check myself from time to time to make sure I'm not putting anything or anyone in the place where God should reign. It can be easy to cross that fine line and allow something to take precedent in our lives but once we realize what is going on, then we must repent of it and welcome God back in His rightful place in our hearts.

As stated before, God is a jealous God and He will have no other gods before Him. To keep things in the right perspective, let this scripture resonate in your heart and mind: *Jesus replied: "Love the Lord your God with all your heart and with all your soul and with all your mind. This is the first and greatest commandment"* Matthew 22:37-38 (NIV). This is how God wants us to love him. Loving God above everyone and everything helps to keep things and people in right perspective in our lives.

When we think of who God is, He is this amazing; self-existent, spiritual being who is the Creator of the universe! He has every right to feel the way He does. NOBODY or NOTHING could ever compare to Him! He deserves to have first place in our hearts. We should set our affections entirely on Him because this all-powerful, all-knowing God whose everywhere at all times, deserves our love on the highest level. There is clearly no other like Him!

When you are idol worshipping, do you not know that in a sense, you are reverencing someone or something with a devotion that belongs only to God? Jesus explains it in this manner in Matthew 6:24 (KJV) *"No man can serve two masters: for either he will hate the one, and love the other; or else he will hold to the one, and despise the other. Ye cannot serve God and mammon"*. If you weighed it out and your preferences are geared toward the idols in your life, you will eventually hate the One and Only True Living God.

In my younger years, I idol worshipped almost everything. Not only did I worship men, I used to also worship my possessions such as my car, my money and clothes. My mind would be so heavily consumed with these things that I thought that I had to have them and I assumed that they could bring me joy. Idols and gods can be anything in our lives from people, to possessions; money; food; relationships; people in the music and entertainment industry, and so on.

We must not be precarious, because to love someone or something more than you love God can be dangerous. It is easy to become lost in anyone or anything that is not of the will of God. As mentioned earlier, when I was in love with someone, they were my whole world and I would allow my days and nights to be consumed with them. At the time, I thought that they were the greatest loves of my life but the LORD eventually gave me a reality check that I so desperately needed.

I was convicted of putting these things before God. I was guilty of loving men more than I loved God. We can tend to give in to the cravings of our flesh and even fall prey to thinking the things we worship can give us all the love and comfort in the world. The lusts of our flesh can lead to the destruction of our souls, but praise God for the forgiveness He has for us all through Christ Jesus.

2 Timothy 3:6 (KJV) *"For of this sort are they which creep into houses, and lead captive silly women laden with sins, led away with divers' lusts."* This also applies to men. Ponder this point, when we give our power over to anything that entertains the flesh, we then succumb to the control of that entity. The spirit within us is already at war with our flesh, therefore, we must not empower the flesh by feeding it with sinful practices.

From our days of youth, we may have had this thirst for inner peace and joy, yet we were naïve and immature. Our flesh were constantly causing us to make unhealthy choices and decisions. Once we gave in to those unhealthy choices, we may have then found ourselves dealing with a crisis and we discovered our tendency to rely on other people to help push us through. Some people tend to turn towards drugs; alcohol; sex; pets; and whatever else they feel will help numb their pain. They seek to find anything to fill the void in their hearts, but none of these things are capable of fixing our issues long term. Some of them may numb the pain for a while but that's just it. It's only a temporary fix, and once the stimulations wear off, you're right back to square one.

Having a right relationship with our LORD Jesus can bring us to a place of healing and deliverance that we so desperately need from time to time in our lives. Only the LORD can truly remove the pain that life brings our way. Only He can bring us true joy, happiness and peace. He can give us joy that the world can't give us, and what the world can't take away.

When our relationship is cultivated with Jesus, and we have matured in the LORD over time, we then come to a place where we realize that no one but our precious Savior can satisfy even our most un-quenchable thirst! John 4:14 (KJV) says, *"But whosoever drinketh of the water that I shall give him shall never thirst; but the water that I shall give him shall be in him a well of water springing up into everlasting life"*. Is your cistern empty? Jesus is offering a drink of water that will give you everlasting life! Let your reservoir become a river of living water, in which your inner man shall never thirst again. You then can receive the power to love God with all of your being!

When God tells us to not have any other gods before Him, He knows exactly what He's doing when He gives us this command. As a loving FATHER, God will establish boundaries; provide discipline; and set rules for His children. He knows our needs and it's important to have boundaries and discipline in our lives to thrive in a healthy place in the LORD Almighty. Think about it, would you give a million dollars to your teenager on their sweet sixteen birthday? No! Why? It is because you, as a good parent know that your child is not ready to take on responsibilities as an adult; the child would become reckless and end up only God knows where.

For this reason, we come to understand that our heavenly FATHER sets boundaries for His children. His love far exceeds the love of earthly parents because He always knows what's best for us. It's not that He doesn't want us to enjoy things in this life; He does not mind blessing us with the desires of our hearts, but He knows how to help us put things into a healthy perspective where we can enjoy them without going overboard.

Speaking of going overboard, here are just a few areas in my life that I once found myself spinning out of control in. For instance, I love food as much as the next person but I used to have such poor self-control over my eating habits. My love for food allowed me to subconsciously pacify myself for whatever the reason. There were days where I was emotional and upset, and I would always turn to food for comfort. I had become so dependent on food to where I became very unhealthy. I was overindulging, which is sinful behavior; I had no self-control, and at the time I did not understand that I was trying to repair and restore myself.

My weight had begun to get out of control due to my eating habits and much to my surprise, I found myself having unwanted conversations with my doctor. The doctor began telling me that I was going to have to start taking medication, but God forbid!!! I do not like, nor have I ever enjoyed taking medication of any kind, therefore I knew that I had to get my emotional eating under control.

Emotional eating was a habit that I could not continue to practice, but my flesh did not want to be defeated. I knew then that I was going to have to change my eating habits but I wasn't sure how. I was depending on food for comfort more than I was depending on God, however, the Spirit within me had to take control. I remember how the LORD began to deal with my mindset regarding food.

He began to show me the kinds of food that were causing damage to my arteries and organs. The foods that I was indulging in were sure to lead to high blood pressure, diabetes, and down the line, possible strokes and heart attacks. As my mindset began to change about food, I began to eliminate certain foods from my diet and I even began to exercise. Through much discipline and commitment of this regimen, I found that I began to feel so much better.

As I began to make healthier decisions about my eating habits, I began to lose weight. Instead of turning to food at my most stressful and emotional times, I found that I could now turn to Jesus. He is able to comfort and sustain me in ways that food never could. I learned how to deal with my issues a lot better, and rather having the issues stress me out, I now practiced turning to the Word of God and praying, and leaving my issues at the altar. Stress would drive me to unhealthy eating and I am now grateful to have this mindset towards food under control. I can now be comforted without having my health put in jeopardy, praise God!

Since changing my eating habits, I am now healthier than I was. I am no longer in any danger of having major health issues. It feels good to now be able to go to the doctor and not be prescribed any medications. I recognized that I have a lot of living to do and if I am to be used by God, I need my body to be in shape to do it. Developing a healthy eating habit is vital to longevity of having a good quality of life.

Our bodies are the temple of the LORD and we must be held accountable to take good care of them. In order for us to be used in a great capacity, we need to be as healthy as we can. When there is something to offset the harmony amongst the systems of our bodies, we will find ourselves stressed out.

If we are impacted by health issues, we can fail at our assigned spiritual tasks, but be encouraged that the LORD can restore you to good health in Christ Jesus. Taking good care of your temple is important. If you are out of control with your eating habits, turn to the LORD who will be glad to help you with the way you view food. He will help you with being in control of how much you eat as well as making healthy choices for what you eat.

The overindulgence of food is but one facet of idolizing. One of the greatest devices of Satan, is to entice people with the love for money. 1 Corinthians 4:2 (KJV), *"Moreover it is required in stewards, that a man be found faithful."* Money was another obstacle for me; I used to have poor self-control in this area of my life as well. All I could think about was having money and having as much of it as I could get, but I found out that my habits with my money was not glorifying God.

I used to have a habit of spending money as fast as I got it. Again, this was another method to pacify myself. For many people, there are some issues that they avoid dealing with, therefore, it is easy to find an outlet to reroute the anxiety, fears, pains, and woes of life. For me, it was shopping, and I would just constantly shop all the time.

I would sometimes jeopardize bills that I knew needed to be paid in order to purchase something that I wanted. I had no discipline in my life when it came to money. I remember thinking, 'God, if only I had a job that paid me more money, but the real issue wasn't that I wasn't making enough money, it was my broken mentality towards the money that I already had.

The resolution was not to make more money, the answer was to come into an alignment with the will of God for my life. Psalm 143:10 (KJV), helps us to beseech the LORD that we may obey Him; *"Teach me to do Thy will; for Thou art my God: Thy spirit is good; lead me into the land of uprightness."* The more the LORD began to deal with my lack to handle the blessing of provision, the more I began to change.

When there is a lack of appreciation for God's hand of provision, it is easy to put earthly desires before Him. The power and prestige of money have destroyed so many men, but why, when Jesus has said in Matthew 19:24 (KJV) *"And again I say unto you, It is easier for a camel to go through the eye of a needle, than for a rich man to enter into the kingdom of God"*. Think on this, since our Holy FATHER owns the cattle on a thousand hills; shall we as His children have lack of anything? No.

My attitude regarding money was neither in alignment with God's blessings, nor His will for me to spend it. When I found myself to be in a rut, I needed to quickly repent and ask of the LORD – have I mishandled something that You trusted me with? It was hard for me to get ahead financially. When I used to emotionally shop, I would end up with so much material stuff that I never needed. Lust of the eyes can be very detrimental to our souls, but thanks be to God that my emotional shopping and my bad habits with money has now been broken.

No longer do I find myself shopping and spending money like there is no tomorrow. I can now differentiate from the things that I need versus my wants. While shopping, I have to ask myself, Henrietta do you really need this or do you just want this? I have to have a reality check with myself so that those bad habits won't resurface.

Today, I am grateful to have a saving mentality instead of a spending mentality. I am saving more money today than I ever have before. I now recognize when there are seasons that I can freely shop without compromising my other responsibilities. Then there are seasons when I need to keep my money in my pocket and save. It is so important to recognize this because some seasons may allow us extra money to spend and shop, and then there are seasons when we need to say no to spending money excessively. Be sure to recognize the season you are in with your money.

The LORD will sometimes test us with our money. If you think about it, how can God give us more if we are not properly managing the little we have? *"He who is faithful in what is least is faithful also in much; and he who is who is unjust in what is least is unjust also in much"* Luke 16:10 (NKJV). This was a wake-up call for me when I knew I needed to do better with my money.

The LORD desires to change our mindset about how we view money and to also take us from constant spending to saving. If we are serious about gaining wealth, we must learn the importance of saving and investing. We must develop a kingdom mentality when it comes to money. Can money become your god? Of course it can. Be wise concerning money. Don't allow yourself to have an obsession with money where you are putting your love for money before your love for God. *"For where your treasure is, there your heart will be also"* Matthew 6:21 (NIV). I believe that God is pleased with us when we exercise wise stewardship over our money. When we have passed the test of money, He can trust us with more of it.

If God leads us daily, we can trust Him to speak to our hearts. Rather than me focusing on obtaining riches given by this world, I prefer to concentrate on the provision of God's hand for my needs. Instead of gaining worldly possessions, I want to be sure that I am serving God with all my being because it is He that hath given me this life to live.

I certainly want to avoid the waste of anything that the LORD has not withheld from me, therefore, I need to seek His direction to see if God has orchestrated a blessing through me for someone else. For I have realized all the things we acquire in the earth is only temporal. It is the relationship between God and His children that is true prosperity.

Money, food, and material things are all perishable; they come and go one way or another, but we have a treasure that is one of a kind, and it is the unconditional love of God. For we can each have our own unique relationship with Him. We do not have to vie for His attention because He watches over each of us. We do not have to brown nose our way to His heart, because He already knows the condition of our hearts. We do not have to persuade Him to fall in love with us, because He already loves us beyond our comprehension.

Having the love of God reign in my heart has allowed me to come to know of real love. If we go back and assess the conditions of some of our past relationships, we can see how multiple times we thought we were in love with someone. We can now identify if it was real love or not. Were you loved as Christ loves the Church? Was there any lack of trust because of certain behaviors? Were you willing to die for the people of your past? Jesus says in John 15:13 (KJV) *"Greater love hath no man than this, that a man lay down his life for his friends."* Yet He died for us all – no love can compare to His love.

There was a time that I had many idols in my heart. They took up so much space in my heart that there was no room for God. As long as those idols were in my heart, I could not love God with all of my heart, my mind, and my soul, but I praise God for deliverance! I am the receiver and reciprocator of His Divine Love!!!

Earlier I spoke of how I used to idolize men and how I felt that I needed validation from a man. Though I no longer believe I need a man to rescue me or validate me, however, he will be required to love me as God stipulates. I can now love him with a healthy dose of love and respect as God intended as well. Therefore, if I am found to be a wife of a man, he must know he has found a good thing, because God is at the core of my heart. His spirit will need to agree with the Spirit that dwells in me.

This amazing love that I have come to experience with the LORD, is truly mind blowing! I am validated as an heir to the Throne of the Most High God! I am validated because the Blood of Jesus was shed for me, to wash away my sins. I am purged and purified, and God sees me clothed in His righteousness. I feel loved because His Spirit transforms me daily to be whole in every way possible. I am experiencing an unconditional love! Don't get me wrong, it's good to be loved by someone and it's good to love, but I feel that there is no love greater than the love of God.

If we tend to put such a high value on people and things and even place them as more important than God, we have now allowed them to dwell in a place in our hearts where they do not belong. We are therefore living out of the will of God and are out of order. When our relationship with the LORD begins to grow deeper, and the love of God begins to flood our hearts like a river, the many things that were out of order in our lives, will now begin to come into perfect alignment. We can then began to see things so much differently.

Money; food; material things; and men, were just a few of the things that had become my god. In hindsight, I understand how much I valued these fleshly desires. I was in a perilous state and did not realize how detrimental it was for my spirit and soul. If there is anything in your life that absorbs your attention; consumes your time; and you have it on a pedestal; reexamine your relationship with the LORD, and redefine your obsessions with these particular things and even people.

Don't be afraid to ask God for help with putting those things that you love in their perspective places. Whatever it is, it doesn't belong in the place where only God should reside. He not only has earned the right to be first in your heart, mind, and soul, but Jesus Christ paid the price for you to have a sacred place in Him.

Jesus is there to help each of us on every level of our lives, no matter the struggle. Be encouraged and know that He is your ever-present Help! There is no appointment needed because He is readily accessible. The very thing that you think He may not be interested in, is the very thing He's interested in helping you with.

Remember, there is no issue too big that God cannot solve, and no issue too small that He doesn't care about, because if it's a concern to you, it's a concern to Him. Never be ashamed to take your issues to the LORD. He cares deeply for you. He is able to handle any problem that you will ever have in this life. When you agree with God of what He knows what's best for you, you will win every time! You are a winner in Christ Jesus! And lastly, remember to love the LORD your God, with all of your heart, your soul, and your mind. Put no one above God.

THERE IS POWER IN UNITY!

During a marriage ceremony, you will normally see the lighting of the unity candles. There will be two candles being joined together to light the third candle which symbolizes the unity of the couple coming together in holy matrimony. It is a sacred moment when a man and woman are united as husband and wife. When the two can honestly encourage and support each other in every way possible throughout their matrimony, it is a wonderful thing. It may start out this way at the beginning of a marriage, but it will take work and dedication to continue.

One of the keys to keeping a healthy relationship is consistency. Being consistent with the acceptance of your spouse, helps the marriage. If from the beginning, that you both can adapt to who each of you are, then you both can be consistent with the acceptance process. Identifying your goals to remain unified is of vital importance. You should set attainable goals to remain unified in your marriage, as well as your family life. Working together while on one accord will be conducive for a healthy life environment, and this includes your financial and ministry goals as well.

There is power in unity! The unity in a marriage is like a strong anchor between a husband and wife; keeping them steady as they go through the storms of life, but the unity between husband, wife and

God is even more powerful and our adversary knows this. That is why he fights so hard to try to keep husband and wife pitted against each other because he knows that the unity between them is a force to be reckoned with.

The Word of God says in Ecclesiastes 4:12, (NLT) *"A person standing alone can be attacked and defeated, but two can stand back-to-back and conquer. Three are even better, for a triple-braided cord is not easily broken"*. For example, if you and your spouse are standing back to back, armed with the armor of God, how can the enemy sneak in and divide and conquer the two of you? It is when you let your guards down against the evil one, that he finds an opportunity to come in between the two of you and wreak havoc on your marriage. Remember, a house divided against itself, cannot stand.

You are never alone in the fight of protecting your marriage; you have God's supernatural strength working with you to fight against the enemy's tactics. You and your spouse are a team, and teams work together to overthrow their components. You are not powerless against the wiles of the devil; but God has given you spiritual weapons to fight with and overcome.

The scripture of John 10:10 (AMP) says that *"The thief comes only in order to steal, and kill, and destroy"*. The enemy seeks to *steal* the longevity of your marriage. He seeks to *kill* the love between a husband and wife. He seeks to *destroy* the union that God has put together, so be aware. Psalm 133:1 (KJV) state, *"Behold, how good and how pleasant it is for brethren to dwell together in unity!"* In other words, there is peace and a pleasantry to experience when the two reside together in harmony.

When spouses are functioning in opposition with each other, the enemy makes his charge. He uses your differences against you both. The adversary will try to trap you in a foothold. If he can cause you to dangle yourself – he will also look for ways to advance against your marriage. Once he is allowed to enter, he will drive an even greater wedge between the two of you, but if you both are unified and on one accord, he doesn't have a chance to destroy the union.

If couples will become familiar with the tactics of the enemy; it shouldn't surprise them when different types of attacks begin to surface within the marriage. Every married couple will go through its ups and downs; that is expected, but remaining unified and being on one accord, you both have the power of the LORD Jesus Christ to help combat the dark forces that comes to test your marriage.

You must remember, you are in a spiritual war with Satan; he is our adversary. During any war there are going to be multiple battles. These can include battles with your stability as a couple, so remember you will combat this attack with faith, love, and truth. Your faith is in a Holy God; if you both love with the love of God in your hearts, His truths will defeat all encounters from the enemy.

You may even encounter battles for the control of your children, but you can combat this by rearing your children with adoration and respect for the will of God in their lives. There may be battles for your home territory; remember to saturate your home with prayers, and practice of God's Word. You both may be faced with the battle for control of your finances; remember God's provision will be sufficient for your needs. Regarding any battles for your health, believe you are the temple of God and use the authority Christ has invested in you to stay healthy.

Have you ever heard of the phrase; "man your battle station"? This instruction is used when you are in combat, therefore, you must be on alert to counterattack the enemy. This is why it is of the most importance to always be prepared with the whole armor of God. You must exercise your God given victory against Satan; his demons, devils, and imps.

Though we have victory – and until there is an order from God to cease fighting; the battles will continue to exist throughout history. We still must be aware of that accusing, lying, and thieving adversary; so in the morning, when you both rise, do an armor check with one another. You can even synchronize your schedules so the enemy cannot attack with accusations of what your spouse could be doing, and so forth. Keep those mental and spiritual frequencies unblocked for open communication. Guard, protect, and warn your spouse to remain alert of any fiery darts.

Activated discernment is also a key factor to identify an opportunity to support unity. When you are engaged in war – both sides will fight until one has been defeated, but here today is your victory!!! Satan has already been defeated and Christ has awarded you both to be more than conquerors in Him!

If there be any miscommunication amongst you two, discern the spirits by what type of spirits they are and their purpose. This will help you to destroy any of their attacks. If perhaps the enemy gets into your camp, be not dismayed, just remember this, Satan does not have the power to foretell anything about your future. Satan can only bring something from your history to complicate your life.

Just know that you have the same information and power to know of the things that have occurred in your past, that caused you pain. Therefore, do not be afraid of your past. You both are starting anew, and if you have already told one another about things that made you ashamed, how then can the enemy defeat you? Satan cannot win!!!

We've all heard the saying, don't go to bed angry with your partner. Whatever misunderstanding occurred, try to forgive whatever has happened to bring an offense against your relationship. If you are not able to resolve it before going to bed, agree to discuss it at a specific time on the following day.

If you do not agree to resolve it, it can spill over into the next day and began to fester and grow deeper and deeper into something that could take weeks or months to deal with. Remember, you must maintain open communication at all costs. If you do not talk about it, you may end up crying, fighting, and screaming about it. Ephesians 4:26-27 (KJV) says, *"Be ye angry, and sin not: let not the sun go down upon your wrath: Neither give place to the devil"*. Once the enemy sees a crack in the door, he will go in.

When there is a breakdown in communication between a husband and wife, the devil will see this as one or both of you becoming vulnerable. For example, if a husband is used to making love to his wife on a regular basis and now she's withholding her love because of disagreements and problems within the marriage, temptation can begin to creep in.

The devil will not recall the Word of God. That is why Christ must remain in the center of the marriage, because the Holy Spirit can convict the wife to help remember her vows as well as the Word of God. Ephesians 5:21 (KJV) *"Submitting yourselves one to another in the fear of God"*. Do not let the enemy use any situation as a temptation to draw an even further wedge between you two.

With having love from his wife withheld, the husband may now be vulnerable and may even be tempted by someone he works with. It could be that very someone who has had her eye on him for quite a while and she has zero respect for him being married, and now all of a sudden, in a moment of weakness, a line has been crossed.

1 Peter 5:8 (KJV) advises, *"Be sober, be vigilant; because your adversary the devil, as a roaring lion, walketh about, seeking whom he may devour"*. When you two are not engaging in sexual intimacy, this is a good time to use for fasting; that way the enemy has no strength to discourage you both in any matter.

Try to resolve your issues with one another quickly so that you both can come back together in unity and be on one accord with each other. When you forgive one another, let go of the offense and do not bring it back up again. We have to keep in mind that when our heavenly FATHER forgives us of our trespasses, He tosses it into the sea of forgetfulness and that is how we have to remember to be with one another.

Find ways to effectively become interwoven. Have discussions that will allow for your growth together. Have discussions about how to raise your family together. Talk about your plans in the event something goes wrong, and have the "what if" conversations. Talk more with one another, and less at one another.

Communication is extremely important in a marriage, and can lead to more things of interest for you both. Try to keep communication open as much as possible, even when it may be difficult to talk about certain things. Poor communication is like a breeding ground for the enemy; it leads to misunderstanding, mistrust, and more problems within the marriage.

Keep God at the center of your marriage. He is already a part of it anyway so don't ignore Him; He is there to help you. *"For the eyes of the LORD run to and fro throughout the whole earth, to shew Himself strong in the behalf of them whose heart is perfect toward Him..."* 2 Chronicles 16:9 (KJV).

The Holy Spirit is there to guide you both in making decisions in your marriage as well on how to love and care for one another. *"With all lowliness and meekness, with longsuffering, forbearing one another in love; Endeavoring to keep the unity of the Spirit in the bond of peace"*. Ephesians 4:2-3 (KJV). God is not surprised at your marital problems; He is there to help the both of you. Whatever decisions that need to be made, lean not to your own understanding as the Word of God tells us but trust God in every aspect of your union.

As your marriage age in number, it's important to remember to make time for one another and not take each other for granted. Find ways to keep the fire going in your marriage because remember, temptation is always lurking around the corner, so find new ways to enjoy the love that you have for one another. Having weekly or bi-weekly date nights is always important. Our lives are often so busy, but be sure not to become too busy where you may begin to neglect your spouse. Take the time to rekindle the romances and remember one another's interest that first attracted you to each other.

There is nothing wrong with being friends with your partner. You should be encouraged to cultivate a great friendship with your spouse. You both should be able to enjoy much fun and laughter with one another from time to time, while also remembering to be kind to one another. We know that overtime, we can become complacent with our partners and even forget to show kindness and respect for one another. It takes work and dedication to keeping the love alive within a marriage but the rewards are so worth it.

A healthy marriage is a marriage that keeps God involved at all times. Staying unified with your spouse will truly help when temptations arise. No marriage is perfect but your marriage stands a chance of overcoming all obstacles when you keep God in the center of it. Keep your union saturated in prayer because a couple who prays together, stays together.

It's going to take something much bigger than just you and your spouse to hold your marriage together, so when you come to the understanding that you both need the help of the LORD Almighty to guide you through this sacred union, the better off you will be. He is Sovereign over the earth, the universe, and over all lives, so allow His power to sustain your lives with one another.

When looking at the word opportunity – this could be your strategy (op), to maintain a safe (port) place for unity.

O = Obey the ways of the LORD and practice His will
P = Plan with one another how to walk as one
P = Pray together, as well as in your alone time with God for each other
O = Openly communicate and be attentive to each other's needs
R = Respect each other's opinions and help each other to grow
T = Trust and believe in God and in your spouse
U = Unify faith and undo any doubts
N = Nullify and identify tactics from the enemy
I = Identify and invalidate enemy attacks, challenges, and hindrances
T = Take the time to spend some time together
Y = Yield unto the LORD for direction and guidance

When you have an opportunity to grow, do not just grow alone, rather grow into and unto one another. The opportunity to use positive strategies will allow you to fight together and not against one another.

Each of these tips can help to aid you in the unity of your marriage. Don't ever forget how sacred and beautiful your union is. Your marriage and the love that you both share is worth fighting for. Marriage is a beautiful depiction of who God is. Take time to remember the covenant agreement that you made with your spouse, because this is not just any relationship, this is *The Covenant Relationship* that involves you, your spouse, and God.

There are days when you may have to think back to *The First Marriage* that took place in the Garden of Eden, when God performed the first ceremony between Adam and Eve. It's good to be reminded of how special and how sacred your union truly is. It is just as special and sacred as Adam and Eve's union was. For that which God has created, He has also ordained. Marriage is an institution established by God and He honors Holy Matrimony.

When you get married, you will be giving your sacred promise before the LORD, and to one another, therefore, be sober and mindful of the <u>The Sacred Vows</u> that you will be professing to the one that you love. Be mindful to take your vows and commitment seriously before the LORD.

I know that while planning a wedding, people can sometimes get so caught up in all of the exciting details but it's good to keep in mind that <u>After A Wedding, Comes A Marriage</u>. Therefore, begin to prepare yourself mentally for everything that will come with this new arrangement in your lives. You are no longer just responsible for just yourself, but you now have a responsibility to love, cherish, and care for your significant other as you confessed in your vows.

<u>Becoming One</u> with your spouse is truly a special time as the both of you are being weaved together into a three strand cord covenant union that cannot be easily broken. You will now become one body; one flesh; but also pray to be one in agreement as you both walk as one.

During times of difficulty in a marriage, we have to be <u>Understanding of The Brokenness We Face</u>. Reflect on your FATHER's grace towards you and your spouse. The more you can grasp about your spouse's internal struggles, the more you can pray about their healing and chances for growth. Try to mirror God and His love in order that they see a God-loving reflection of themselves when they look into you.

Try to also keep in mind that it is not good to view your partner as your enemy. It is good to develop an understanding of <u>Spiritual Wickedness In High Places</u> to be able to use wisdom and properly prepare your-self to combat the real enemy who comes only to try to steal, kill, and destroy marriages; but greater is He who is in you, than he who is in the world!

For those who are currently single, remember to be patient because seasons will change, so just simply <u>Give Yourself Permission to Be Single</u> and experience the goodness of God during those times when it's just you and Him. There is so much living to do while discovering who you are in Christ Jesus and discovering what you were created for, all while waiting to meet the right one.

Whether you are dating, or already married, remember to <u>Put No One Above God</u>. Loving God with all of your heart, soul, and mind will help you to keep people and even things in their perspective places in your life. As amazing and awesome as our God is, He deserves to have first place in our hearts above anyone and anything.

And finally, remember that <u>There Is Power in Unity</u> between a husband and wife. You both can overcome the tactics of the enemy and achieve some amazing things together. Explore and experience all areas of your lives, and learn the power of walking as one. You both are now unified and can allow the Holy Spirit to guide you through your journey of marriage. With God at the center of your union, your marriage can withstand the winds of life as they may come. Couples that have their marriage anchored in the LORD can defeat the odds! Your union is beautiful and sacred, therefore, be sure to love and care for one another deeply.

BIOGRAPHY

Henrietta Freeman was born and raised in Greenville, South Carolina, where she grew up with five other siblings in the heart of Greenville County. She earned an Associate's Degree at ECPI College of Technology. She is the mother of two young adults; a facilitator, and an entrepreneur. Henrietta is an ordained Minister. She is also the Author of previous book, *"Guard Your Heart with All Diligence, for Out of the Heart Flows the Issues of Life."*

Henrietta is the Founder of Healing Waters CAW (Center for Abused Women). She is a survivor and speaker on domestic violence. If you or someone you know is involved in a domestic violence situation, or an abusive relationship, please seek help immediately! For more info regarding the committed work that we do at Healing Waters (CAW) please visit the website at www.healingwaterscaw.org.

Henrietta is passionate about helping and encouraging others through her ministry work; her writing, and speaking engagements. It gives her great joy to witness change come about in other people's lives for the better, all through Christ Jesus! She credits her LORD, Jesus Christ for all that He has helped her to overcome, and for using her story for His glory!

BIOGRAPHY

Lightning Source UK Ltd.
Milton Keynes UK
UKHW022132060223
416584UK00024B/449